The *LoveSpell* Experiment

My Year Exploring Love
&
Discovering A Secret To Happiness

I. J. Weinstock

For information write:

DreaMaster Books

Online at:

DreaMasterBooks@gmail.com

www.IJWeinstock.com

Cover art by Christina WS
Layout services by EditWriteDesign.com

For Joy,

*who continually teaches me greater
and greater lessons of love.*

For Lilly,

*who holds my hand and my heart and
who helps me play more love into the world.*

For Oprah,

*who's inspired so much love in the world
and who knows the LoveSpell Secret.*

Because what you focus on expands,
when you focus on the goodness in your life,
you create more of it.

— Oprah Winfrey

Contents

Part 1: Introduction

Part 2: The Experiment

August

September

October

November

December

Part 3: Epilogue

Part 4: The Results

Part 1

Introduction

Love is everywhere

but most of us are blind to it.

Romance is just one aspect of love.

Our primary relationship is with ourselves.

— Marianne Williamson

(What Do You) *Love is the Answer*

Poets, philosophers and pop songs praise love. Even the Bible proclaims *Love is the answer*. I discovered the profound truth of what for many is a cliché in the most unlikely way.

On New Year's Eve I attended a drum circle to ring in 2012. I sat in a Long Island living room with a dozen other people, beating a hand-held Native American drum in the traditional heartbeat rhythm. Ba*bam*! Ba*bam!* The room vibrated with the booming beat of the 12 drums that mimicked our hearts and soon became hypnotic. That's when it happened—I heard my late wife, Joy, ask me a question which changed my life.

This wasn't the first time I'd received communications from the Afterlife. In fact, I wrote a grief memoir—*JOYride: How My Late Wife Loved Me Back To Life*—about Joy's spirit leading me on an incredible journey to heal my grief after her death on Good Friday, 2007.

The question Joy asked me on that fateful New Year's Eve was simple yet profound:

What do you love?

As if in answer, I began beating the drum for all the things that I loved.

- **I love ceremony and celebration.**
- **I love being among kindred spirits.**
- **I love banging a drum!**

By the end of the drum circle, I'd made a new year's resolution to *beat the drum for love* all year. For me, 2012 would be *The Year of Love*.

Every day via my Twitter account @SoulmateGuider I declared—in 140 characters or less—something I loved. And so began my *LoveSpell Experiment.*

The Subject: From Oy to Joy

It's ironic that a child of Holocaust survivors, born in a refugee camp, raised with tales of unspeakable Nazi horrors, SS atrocities and death camps would subject himself to a *LoveSpell Experiment.*

And perhaps not. To emerge from the shadow of the Holocaust, I had to climb out of the darkest depths into the heights. From Oy to Joy! Literally.

I met Joy in the mid-90's. We were so happy we wanted to help other people find the love of their dreams. So we created a day-long workshop called 12 Steps to Finding Your Soulmate which we led in Los Angeles where we lived.

When I lost Joy to breast cancer, I was devastated. I didn't know if life was worth living. But a remarkable thing happened—Joy led me on an extraordinary journey to heal my grief. Inspired by my experience, I've written several books about healing from loss and share what I've learned by leading workshops at bereavement conferences.

The Challenge

On that fateful New Year's Eve when my *LoveSpell Experiment* began, I was in the fourth year of rebuilding my life after the devastation of losing Joy to cancer. I had been blessed with a great love. The price of such great love, I discovered, is profound grief.

I'd had a varied career in the arts—actor, artist, author, producer—with highs and lows, successes and failures. While I cared for Joy during her six-year struggle with cancer, I neglected my career. Now, at the age of sixty, I faced the formidable challenge of reinventing myself.

I was taken to that New Year's Eve drum circle by Lilly Julien, a wonderful woman with whom I'd been developing a bi-coastal relationship. With increasing frequency we traveled back and forth between LA and LI to be with each other. The 3,000 mile distance between us was overcome by the passion and purpose we shared.

Lilly, a painter and sculptor, had also known great loss. Her 20-year-old daughter had been in a fatal car accident 20 years earlier, and her husband had suffered a massive heart attack eight years later. Like me, she'd also been inspired by "signs" from her loved ones. A dream visitation from her daughter became the inspiration for a non-profit grief organization called COPE that she founded to support families who've lost a child in the

New York metropolitan area. Both Lilly and I realized that when you share passion *and* purpose, you've found a soulmate.

As we rang in the New Year 2012, I was poised for a major life change—if I was going to create a new life with Lilly, we had to be together. It became increasingly obvious that *I* had to be the one to move, since she was tied to Long Island by her family (two children, grandchildren an elderly mother) as well as her grief organization.

Leaving sunny southern California where I'd lived happily and joyfully for nearly twenty-five years for the cold of a northeast winter was the last thing I'd imagined myself doing. Saying goodbye to wonderful friends and the loving community Joy and I had cultivated was painful even to contemplate. But we do crazy things for love.

I spent more and more time (often months!) with Lilly in LI, living out of a suitcase. It became increasingly difficult to leave her to go back to California. And each time I returned to LA, my home seemed stranger and stranger to me. Understandably, since my home was no longer where my heart was.

Like most people, I was resistant to change, especially to leaving the home in which I'd experienced so much happiness with Joy. At some point, I knew I would have to make a decision. Fortunately, as a writer I could work anywhere. Presenting workshops at bereavement conferences didn't depend on where I lived. With no children and both parents deceased, I was much freer than Lilly. And so I would be the one to move.

According to psychologists, a major move—like the cross-country one I faced, uprooting myself from a place I'd lived in and loved for so many years—is one of life's greatest stressors. Just below death and divorce. A mini-death of sorts.

As the clock struck midnight and everyone shouted "Happy New Year!", the inevitable ordeal and upheaval of my move loomed before me.

Part 2

The Experiment

What follows is a record of what I ultimately called my *LoveSpell Experiment.* It's a very intimate document—that's what love requires.

Someone else's *LoveSpell Experiment* will be very different—an intimate reflection of them.

Every *LoveSpell Experiment* is uniquely personal. Yet the results, I believe, will be the same—greater love, health and happiness.

JANUARY

1. I love candlelight, moonlight, the spotlight.

2. I love walking, stretching, dancing.

3. I love a good yawn, a loud sigh & a deep breath.

4. I love birdsong in the morning. I love dreaming. I love a hot shower.

5. I love remembering great memories from my past, my passions and even my passwords.

6. I love daydreaming, fantasizing, imagining the best of all possible worlds.

7. I love horseplay, foreplay and wordplay.

8. I love stroking my dog, stroking my lover and stroking myself.

9. I love singing, daydreaming and free-associating in the shower.

10. I love the word "and" because it's one of the most hopeful words in the English language.

11. I love looking at reflections in water, in mirrors and in glass.

12. I love when people put their creed into their deeds & commit random acts of kindness.

13. I love swinging a tennis racket, a baseball bat and my dance partner.

14. I love walks in the morning, movies in the afternoon and parties at night.

15. I love the bare trees in winter, the beautiful lines their leafless branches make.

16. I'm flying to LA and love looking at the clouds, eating the snacks on Jet Blue, and the wheels touching down.

17. I love the view from my LA window of palm trees waving in the breeze.

18. It's my Bday! I love my life—the "good" & "bad," the loves and losses—and my Mom, may she rest in peace, who brought me into this world.

Happiness is anyone and anything
that's loved by you.

— Charles M. Schulz

In the Beginning...

Early in January, I left Lilly and traveled back to LA. Still inspired by Joy's communication, I kept my New Year's resolution and continued my daily declarations of love.

During our life together Joy taught me so much about love—most importantly, how much I could love! After she was gone, her spirit continued teaching me even greater lessons about love—that it's *all* a gift: the love *and* the loss. If answering her New Year's Eve question *What Do I Love?* was my next lesson in love, I wanted to do my homework.

Every day I took a few minutes to declare a few loves on Twitter with the intention of collecting 1001 over the course of the year. For some reason I found declaring three loves easier than just one. Perhaps it took the pressure off that one love being so precious.

JANUARY

19. I love playing hide-and-seek with a child, with my dreams, with God.

20. I love sunsets and the orgasmic explosion of colors that fades into the darkness of night.

21. I love seeing old friends, hearing their good news & celebrating someone's dream-come-true.

22. I love LOSING myself in the dance and FINDING myself in the stillness of meditation

23. I love having my feet on the ground, my head in the clouds and the sun on my face.

24. I love dancing in the dark, singing in the rain and counting my blessings.

25. I love standing up for myself, for another, for what's right.

26. I love people who are inspired to strip away their facades, their defenses, even their clothes.

27. I love the sound of chimes, the smell of thyme & the satisfaction of rhymes.

28. I love birds in flight, Lady Justice doing right, and the pen making might.

29. I love scratching an itch, throwing a pitch, feeling enriched.

30. I love listening to music with my hips, leaving big tips, watching a beautiful woman apply color to her lips.

31. I love that the stars have no number, the sea has no rest and love has no limits.

32. I love yawning, howling, Wow-ing.

33. I love those breathtaking moments when my "blood turns to wine" and I feel so ALIVE!

34. I love long kisses & short skirts, high marks & low interest rates.

35. I love getting up after I've fallen down.

How do I love thee?

Let me count the ways.

—Elizabeth Barrett Browning

First Traps & Obstacles

Instinctively, the writer in me stepped forward. I tried to be poetic, using rhythm and rhyme and the power of threes. And I began to feel like I was writing a love poem—

How Do I Love Me?
Let Me Count the Ways?

But that soon got old. If I was going to try to write an epic love poem, there was no way I could or would sustain it. The literary merits of my love declarations were incidental, and poetry was probably an obstacle to the simple act of answering Joy's question.

I had so many simple loves—my down pillow, a hot shower, chocolate-covered espresso beans. Why not just acknowledge them? Instead of a poem, how about a list?

JANUARY

36. I love my down comforter and pillow.

37. I love my coffee in the morning and reading something interesting that gives me an AHA!

38. I love starting up conversations with strangers and discovering what we have in common.

39. I love exercising my body and my imagination, but not at the same time.

40. I love feeding the ducks & geese & seagulls at the Lake, even though you're not supposed to.

41. I love eating popcorn in the movies and getting the salt just right.

42. I love watching my team win, especially when they come from behind.

43. I love hunting for the freshest food at the market by searching the expiration and sell-by dates.

44. I love cleaning and drying my ears with a Q-tip after I shower.

45. I love having something to look forward to every day.

46. I love taking a nap in the afternoon, especially if I didn't sleep much the night before.

47. I love looking through old photos and remembering where and who I've been...and with whom.

48. I love the feeling of being in the flow that I get from doing Tai Chi.

49. I love seeing rainbows, which I did this morning.

50. I love the feeling of peace & calm that I experience whenever I do alternate nostril breathing.

51. I love eyes because they're always naked.

JANUARY

52. I love watching hawks circling round & round on thermals.

53. I love that moment when the sun comes out and everything seems possible.

54. I love to snack on fresh pineapple and Trader Joe's peanut butter-filled pretzels, but not too often.

55. I love the way clouds form & reform into endless shapes.

56. I love squeezing the last bit of toothpaste out of the tube for days and even weeks.

57. I love crop circles because they defy interpretation and are a true Mystery that blows my mind.

58. I love having a great customer service experience when I call with a problem and they really help.

59. I love the rare times I wake up early enough to watch the sunrise like I did this morning.

60. I love feeling that I can make a difference—in one person's life and even in the world.

61. I love feeling at the end of the day I've accomplished a lot & that I'm closer to realizing my dream.

62. I love remembering loved ones who've passed on and experiencing the truth that Love is Eternal.

63. I love the optimistic view of our romance with digital technology that ends "App-ily Ever After."

64. I love throwing a bunch of leftovers in a pot and making a delicious soup.

65. I love being curious and not knowing...so that I can be surprised.

66. I love watching the ducks, geese & egrets at the lake and being transported into their world

67. I love having NOTHING to do and thinking EVERYTHING is possible.

Let yourself be silently drawn

by the stronger pull of what you really love.

— Rumi

Priming the LovePump

I soon found that, stressed by the hectic demands of daily life, there were times I couldn't come up with things I loved. That's when I discovered that love is like a well that sometimes has to be primed so that the precious substance can be pumped to the surface of one's awareness.

If I first focused on easy things to love—family, children, pets, my favorite team, a wonderful memory from the past—the simple act of thinking about them brought a smile to my face and a warmth to my heart. That was the place to start.

On those stressed-out days when finding something in my life to love seemed impossible, I spent a few minutes priming the *LovePump*, as it were. Once the love began to flow, it was much easier to find other things in my life that I loved.

JANUARY

68. I love mornings when the day stretches out before me and my optimism is at its height.

69. I love avocados—in my salads & as guacamole mixed with pineapple salsa.

70. I love BREATHING—inhaling nourishing oxygen-prana, exhaling & eliminating carbon dioxide-toxins.

71. I love the anticipation of Super Bowl Sunday especially when my team is playing.

72. I love finishing projects because it's so much harder than starting them.

73. I love buying EXPERIENCES rather than THINGS—that's how I grow my soul.

74. I love DREAMING so much that even if I wake up from a bad dream, I want to go back to continue it.

75. I love having a WHY in life because then I can deal with any WHAT & HOW.

76. I love feeding seagulls when they hover in the air above me and catch the food I throw up to them.

77. I love OVERDOING the things worth overdoing, especially when it comes to love.

78. I love seeing/feeling the connection between ideas-things-people—the ONENESS.

79. I love giving someone a "melting hug."

80. I love the Everything feeling of wanting Nothing.

81. I love the silence of early morning's birdsong before the noise of my To-Dos.

82. I love being asked a thought-provoking, soul-searching question, so I can discover more of myself.

83. I love HUNGER in all its forms because it makes satisfying it so DELICIOUS.

JANUARY

84. I love helping people focus on the bright side of life.

85. I love wearing a red clown nose that makes children happy.

86. I love being visited by a great IDEA because it feels so good, almost like sex.

87. I love to live out loud even when I retreat into my silence.

88. I love shaving with a new sharp razor blade and walking in old comfortable shoes.

89. I love trading my cleverness & wit for wonder & amazement.

90. I love eggs—scrambled, omelet, over-easy, even huevos rancheros.

91. I love the sparkling iridescent colors on a mallard duck's neck.

92. I love the deep tissue massage I received today—Ouch! No pain, no gain!

93. I love being wise about some things and silly about others.

94. I love playing "devil's advocate" to stimulate a good conversation.

95. I love movies that surprise me, yet I love seeing some movies again & again.

96. I love how declaring 3 "things I love" helps neutralize any negative thought.

97. I love the lettuce wraps at PF Chang's.

98. I love "synchronicities" or as some people call them "coincidences."

99. I love full moons, especially at moonrise when it looks so incredibly big!

100. I love blowing bubbles—for the children in my life & the child in me.

101. I love the way a sunny day feels after a rainy one.

The flow of water carves rock, a little bit at a time.

And our personhood is carved, too,

by the flow of our habits.

— Jonathan Safran Foer

A Love Habit

By February, when most New Year's resolutions fall by the wayside, I realized that I'd developed a habit—a *Love Habit*. Like brushing my teeth, I felt strange not declaring a few *new* loves every day.

Also, I noticed a subtle shift taking place within me. I became more aware of just how many different things I loved. I collected loves like beautiful shells on a beach. And the more loves I found, the more I could see. The more I saw, the better I felt.

Something powerful was happening. So I began to do some research hoping to understand what I was experiencing.

FEBRUARY

102. I love anticipating the arrival of my TweetHeart who's on a plane to LA.

103. I love looking at my life with my heart instead of my head.

104. I love kissing my TweetHeart after being apart for 3 weeks.

105. I love the 4-letter word "slow" when it comes to breathing, eating & sex.

106. I love the people in my life who scratch an itch I can't reach.

107. I love feeling with my heart because thinking is at the root of all stress.

108. I love bouncing on my rebounder in the AM, on my workout ball in the PM, and on my bed with my Baby at night.

109. I love sitting at an outdoor cafe, sipping coffee & watching the world go by.

110. I love swinging in my hammock, feeling soothed as if rocked in a cradle.

111. I love hearing that I've inspired someone and made a difference in their life.

112. I love being the "poster child" for the human-at-play.

113. I love AHAs, mine or somebody else's.

114. I love the color turquoise almost as much as the color green.

115. I love napping on a bench at the lake as the sun sets.

116. I love stretching in the shower while the hot water massages my muscles.

117. I love water: drinking it, watching it, swimming & floating in it.

118. I love that magical moment when there's a break in the clouds.

119. I love dreaming of a better world and playing it into reality.

120. I love having friends over for dinner and getting drunk on our laughter.

FEBRUARY

121. I love participating in Native American ceremony because it reminds me that everything is alive.

122. I love seeing a good movie that transports me into another world.

123. I love the intoxication of flowers: their beauty, fragrance & sensuality.

124. I love hearing from old friends and "reeling in the years."

125. I love jumping on my trampoline in the morning 108 times.

126. I love taking a nap on a rainy day.

127. I love wearing my black leather sport jacket out at night.

128. I love burying my face in newly blooming purple wisteria and inhaling its fragrance.

129. I love rolling on the floor with children and laughing til it hurts.

130. I love realizing that the older I get, the more I say "I used to..."

131. I love seeing the first buds of the cherry blossoms.

132. I love eating chocolate especially the dark kind, because it's like eating love.

133. I love thinking that an EKG tests my heart by measuring my Empathy, Kindness & Gratitude.

134. I love how the great yogi described the 5th level of realization—"Everything becomes hilarious!" Where do I sign up?

135. I love this Wayne Dyer quote—"If you change the way you look at things, the things you look at change."

136. I love my TweetHeart telling me this morning that last night I woke up just to say "I love you."

137. I love the irony that camouflage is the new fashion rage for men—hiding when you want to be seen!

There is no such thing as an idle thought.

All thought creates form on some level.

Every thought leads to either love or fear.

— A Course in Miracles

The Quantum Effect

Metaphysics and quantum physics both maintain that whatever you put your attention on expands. In the same way that a magnifying glass makes everything appear bigger or can focus the rays of the sun to ignite a fire, whatever you focus your awareness on grows.

Neuroscience has confirmed that when you become consciously aware of any enjoyment, you amplify and magnify the experience. The study of positive psychology has discovered that when you prioritize love and other positive emotions, you actually get more of them.

Here was scientific validation for the prescription to *count my blessings* and *beat the drum for love.*

FEBRUARY

138. I love waking up from a bad dream cuz I remember nightmarish times in my life when I wished I was dreaming but couldn't wake up.

139. I love stories that begin with the words "Once upon a time..."

140. I love finding a mistake in a bill & saving myself $150!

141. I love having some good TV shows to watch on my DVR.

142. I love seeing a "seed" I've planted begin to bloom.

143. I love finally having paid my bills after procrastinating as much as I can.

144. I love seeing old friends and getting caught up on their new adventures.

145. I love putting a new blade in my razor & rebooting my computer.

146. I love the way Valentine's Day focuses us on who and what we love.

147. I love stimulating conversations that trigger new ideas.

148. I love surprise parties, but only if I've had a shower and brushed my teeth.

149. I love watching people dance & then doing their "dance" as a way to get to know them.

150. I love finding pennies in the street, nickels & dimes, too.

151. I love seeing butterflies alight on a flower and open their beautiful wings.

152. I love my dishwasher and toaster oven!

153. I love sharing the blessings in my life with my friends.

154. I love adjusting my car mirrors so that I don't have a blind spot.

155. I love looking at photos of friends and family.

156. I love walking a different way to the same old place—it becomes an adventure.

FEBRUARY

157. I love the sacred, the mundane and even the profane.

158. I love the classical music of Bach and Chopin.

159. I love having a sense of humor and laughing whenever I can.

160. I love how people's lives can either be viewed as "role models" or "cautionary tales."

161. I love weekends because I can devote more of my time to what I love.

162. I love living in LA with its sunny weather, palm trees, mountains and ocean.

163. I love that there are so many great 4-letter words—hope, kind, good, give & love, to name a few.

164. I love being able to admit that there've been times in my life when I haven't acted kindly or generously—and forgiving myself.

165. I love reading my old journals to see who I once was and how much I've grown.

166. I love the idea of infinite possibilities and letting that guide my actions.

167. I love being intoxicated by the fragrance of night-blooming jasmine.

168. I love stories about overcoming adversity—turning tragedy into triumph.

169. I love watching hummingbirds hover next to their feeders.

170. I love my car and the reliability, convenience and freedom it gives me.

171. I love the feeling of a cool breeze on a warm day.

172. I love Fridays—TGIF—a feeling of completion and anticipation.

173. I love getting lost in work because then it's become play.

1001 Names for Love

We usually associate the word "love" with our feelings for another. But Joy asked me *what* I loved, not *who* I loved.

As I continued declaring what I loved, I thought about the word *love*. And its limitations. I came across this fascinating observation by the renowned psychologist Robert Johnson.

> *"Sanskrit has 96 words for love; ancient Persian has 80, Greek three, and English only one. This is indicative of the poverty of awareness or emphasis that we give to that tremendously important realm of feeling. Eskimos have 30 words for snow, because it is a life-and-death matter to them to have exact information about the element they live with so intimately. If we had a vocabulary of 30 words for love ... we would immediately be richer and more intelligent in this human element so close to our heart. An Eskimo probably would die of clumsiness if he had only one word for snow; we are close to dying of loneliness because we have only one word for love. Of all the Western languages, English may be the most lacking when it comes to feeling."*

The dictionary lists these synonyms for the verb to *love*:

> *admire, adulate, be attached to, be captivated by, be crazy about, be enamored of, be enchanted by, be fascinated with, be fond of, be in love with, canonize, care for, cherish, choose, deify, delight in, dote on, esteem, exalt, fall for, fancy, glorify, have affection for, hold dear, hold high, idolize, long for, lose one's heart to, prefer, prize, put on pedestal, think the world of, thrive with, treasure, venerate, worship....*

I realized that Joy's question—"*What* do you love?" rather than "*Who* do you love?"— had sent me on a quest that was expanding my notion of love.

Love isn't just something we feel
for others, it's who we are.
Love is actually the substance,
the building blocks,
the essence of everything in our lives.
We're made up of love.
Our molecules are formed from love.
We are love.

— Marci Shimoff

FEBRUARY

174. I love real-life ironies: a Weight Watchers office above a Baskin Robbins; a Psychic Fair that's "cancelled due to unforeseen circumstances."

175. I love forgetting some things so I can be reminded of them all over again.

176. I love skylights—they bring the sky inside and light up my life.

177. I love that the Greeks called the force that binds the universe together Eros, another term for love.

178. I love dark chocolate-covered espresso beans—for the taste and the caffeine rush.

179. I love being inspired by the beauty of the female body.

180. I love that Eskimos have lots of names for "snow"—we need lots of names for "love."

181. I love running water, flush toilets and electricity 24/7.

182. I love to think that God has billions of eyes through which we see ourselves.

183. I love Saturdays—the weekend stretching out before me.

184. I love all sorts of creating—from Art to Zaniness—because we are creators.

185. I love re-interpreting the "story" of my life with a new "happy ending."

186. I love moving my body—swimming, dancing, yoga-ing and lovemaking.

187. I love listening to music with my ass instead of my ears and moving to the rhythm.

188. I love Sundays yet feel wistful and saddened by the gathering sunset of the weekend.

189. I love the Oscars—like the Super Bowl, it brings us all together declaring what we love.

FEBRUARY

190. I love how sometimes I can't tell the difference between the movies I've seen & my own memories.

191. I love finding new things to be grateful for—I'm a Gratitude Hunter.

192. I love the smell of newly cut grass, especially in the morning.

193. I love when my plane takes off but even more when it touches down.

194. I love how sharing something I've experienced can open up new possibilities for someone else.

195. I love how well I sleep knowing how difficult it can be for some people.

196. I love stopping to smell the roses, literally & metaphorically—Ahhhh!

197. I love my body—how well it's aged, how athletic & rhythmic & pain-free.

198. I love seeing new buds on tree branches, signs of hope and possibility.

199. I love the beauty of swans, their long graceful necks & black-masked eyes.

200. I love baptizing myself in the shower every morning.

201. I love blessing my food before I eat.

202. I love discovering new things about myself.

203. I love swinging on my hammock basking in the sun.

204. I love walking downhill after I've walked uphill.

205. I love collaborating on a creative project.

206. I love giving presents to children.

207. I love watching people love their pets.

208. I love those moments—like now—when my dog comes over & licks my typing hand.

209. I love the topsy-turvy possibilities of Leap Day—doing the OPPOSITE of what's usually done like WOMEN ASKING MEN OUT.

Plant impossible gardens.

Look forward to dreams.

Cry during movies.

Swing as high as you can on a swing set.

Cultivate moods. Do it for love.

Take lots of naps.

Take moon baths. Giggle with children.

Listen to old people.

Entertain your inner child.

Build a fort with blankets.

Get wet. Hug trees. Write love letters.

— Sark

The Rainbow of Love

I began to view the full spectrum of love like a musical chord composed of different notes or a rainbow composed of different colors. Most of us call the color red "love" and the other colors we call *like*, *enjoy*, *delight*, etc.

Beyond romantic and interpersonal love, there's the love that thrills us when we're moved by music; the love that brings us to tears of recognition by great tales told in books and movies; and of course, the love that takes our breath away.

These are the great oaks, evergreens and redwoods of love. And yet, the daffodils, daisies and even the grasses of love are equally important. Our lives are filled with subtle loves—pleasures, enjoyments, satisfactions—that we savor, that are unique to us, and that make life worth living.

There's love in a garden tended, in something broken mended. There's love in duty, in honor, in kindness. There's obviously love in a kiss, but also in a hug, a pat on the shoulder, a handshake. The world is full of expressions of love.

Our lives are not lived only through great loves, but rather through the small daily loves that are the building blocks of a happier life.

MARCH

210. I love being "tickled" in just the right way.

211. I love how children help us not take life so seriously.

212. I love watching people greeting each other in airports.

213. I love kissing—especially with a good kisser—it's amazing what you can do with your mouth.

214. I love road trips, especially with someone I love riding shotgun.

215. I love driving over the Chesapeake Bay Bridge-Tunnel for 21 miles.

216. I love watching tall grasses 10 ft high waving in the breeze.

217. I love hearing about the "signs" people have received from their departed loved ones.

218. I love the paradox that "success" often hides inside of "failure" but you have to keep your eyes open & keep going!

219. I love when people turn their loss into a legacy that inspires others.

220. I love a good salsa that makes everything taste better.

221. I love hearing inspiring stories of animal-human communication.

222. I love walking the beach especially at low tide.

223. I love sauerkraut on my hot dogs.

224. I love contemplating life from the perspective of death.

225. I love declaring things I love, especially on days I don't feel that good.

226. I love leftovers, especially when I don't feel up to preparing a meal.

227. I love being able to choose where to put my attention and today I choose to focus on what I love.

MARCH

228. I love when shafts of sunlight light up my life and create a still-life work of art.

229. I love feeling better today than I did yesterday and anticipating feeling even better tomorrow.

230. I love watching flames flicker in the fireplace.

231. I love seeing how creative people can be with pizza!

232. I love seeing the love we share become art in my lover's sculptor hands.

233. I love how reworking something over & over makes it even better. Yet there's always the danger of reworking it to death!

234. I love eating, especially when I'm hungry, famished, STARVING!

235. I love how necessity is the mother of invention and how deadlines focus the mind.

236. I love finding something I thought I'd lost.

237. I love cookies—chocolate chip, oatmeal raisin & almond.

238. I love flowers, even though I don't know most of their names.

239. I love overhead fans because they circulate the air I breathe and hypnotize my mind.

240. I love a good stretch, just like a cat or dog.

241. I love sipping coffee in the morning while reading emails.

242. I love daydreaming on a road trip—miles, music & memories.

243. I love mirrors, especially distorted ones that make me laugh.

244. I love lying on the ground looking at a blue sky through pink cherry blossom-filled branches.

245. I love watching new parents play rock-paper-scissor to decide who's going to change their baby's diaper.

The heart is like a garden.

It can grow compassion or fear, resentment or love.

What seeds will you plant there?

— Jack Kornfield

The Heart vs. the Mind

After reading studies that the heart generates a greater magnetic field than the brain—5,000 times stronger!—I began thinking about the heart, the organ of love, versus the mind.

The heart is the first organ created from the fertilized egg as it begins to grow into a human fetus. The heart originates before the brain. Does that make the heart primary? The mind can get lost in a hall of mirrors of its own making. Perhaps the heart is a truer compass.

I was surprised to learn that the second organ which develops in the human embryo after the heart is the tongue. Perhaps that's why it's so powerful to declare what you love!

MARCH

246. I love how the phrase "leave them to their own devices" has become so literal & so apt a description of current child-rearing.

247. I love the sound of water—at the ocean, by a stream, from a fountain.

248. I love exploring the inner frontiers of my mind.

249. I love people expressing their unique talent.

250. I love making fog on windows & mirrors with my breath, then drawing with my finger.

251. I love "happy accidents," when the mistake turns into the perfect solution.

252. I love "lazy Sundays" when the weather is lousy and sleeping in feels great.

253. I love remembering something from my childhood, like how I stirred my ice cream into a softy.

254. I love getting together with childhood friends and feeling how far we've come.

255. I love to wonder who I'd be without my memories—forget amnesia, would I even be me?

256. I love even my "pet peeves"—like drivers who don't use their turn signals.

257. I love finally realizing that a disappointment was ultimately in my best interests.

258. I love this statistic—more people are injured on toilets than by skiing.

259. I love looking out of a plane's window at a city lit up at night.

260. I love arriving home after a long trip and falling into bed.

261. I love the stark contrast of seeing a flower bloom on a cactus.

262. I love getting so quiet that I can feel the blood rushing through my veins.

263. I love playing with children because most adults are so boring!

MARCH

264. I love seeing bees drinking nectar out of flowers, especially now with so many hives dying.

265. I love being showered by cherry blossoms that the breeze blows off the trees.

266. I love figuring things out, having the light bulb go on, being inspired.

267. I love using the 20% discount coupons I get in the mail at Bed Bath & Beyond.

268. I love looking at the pink azaleas blooming on my patio.

269. Sometimes I love being alone so I can experience my Self without any distractions.

270. I love finally catching up on all the mail that's piled up since I've been away.

271. I love dancing—moving my body to the rhythm, to the beat!

272. I love making a child laugh.

273. I love dissolving my Ego occasionally & tuning in to the Oneness.

274. I love my iPod and the way it helps me manage my music and mood.

275. I love living in LA where the temperature today is 79' and it's dry!

276. I love doing new things, but I also love doing old familiar things, too.

277. I love hearing that my 89 year-old uncle still dances several times a week.

278. I love lying under a blooming pear tree & looking up at the birds & bees.

279. I love wondering if our so-called "connectivity" is an illusion paradoxically creating more loneliness.

280. I love looking around my home and seeing things I love to look at!

281. I love slowing down through yoga & meditation so I feel the sensation of my aliveness as pure joy.

I celebrate myself, and sing myself.

— Walt Whitman

A Song of Myself

Lilly lives around the corner from Walt Whitman's birthplace. The poet's name is on roads, shops and even malls. The highest point on the island is a wooded hill nearby where Whitman and now I often walked. On the summit sits a huge boulder with one of Whitman's poems inscribed on it. Walt Whitman is *everywhere!*

Not surprisingly, as the months passed, and I declared more and more things I loved, I sometimes thought of my Experiment as a *Song of Myself* (to borrow the title of Whitman's great epic poem).

As I wrote this Song of Myself day after day, I discovered things about myself I hadn't realized. In mining my life for things that I loved, I uncovered precious jewels. It was like finding buried treasure.

As my inventory of loves grew, I became aware of an additional benefit of this experiment—the evolving self-portrait. When I re-read the loves I'd collected, it was as if I was looking at myself in a special mirror and I began to see myself in surprising ways. A new self-portrait emerged, painted from the brushstrokes of what I loved.

So not only did I benefit from the process of casting a *LoveSpell*, but the product of my *LoveSpell Experiment*—a self-portrait, a "love portrait"—enriched my life as well.

MARCH

282. I love having a heart-to-heart that clears the air and soothes hurt feelings.

283. I love feeling the release when I stretch and do a forward bend.

284. I love watching a blue heron spread its huge wings as it glides to a landing.

285. I love my blender and juicer to make healthy smoothies and veggie drinks.

286. I love standing still in the shower & letting my imagination run wild.

287. I love how much better I feel after a good night's sleep.

288. I love seeing people enjoying a Sunday in the park with their families.

289. I love turning my back to the sun and seeing what kind of shadow I make.

290. I love the t-shirt that says "I only look like I'm a good time."

291. I love walking barefoot—in the grass, on the beach—feeling the grounding beneath my feet.

292. I love putting on clean underwear after taking a shower.

293. I love standing on the bridge over the creek and feeling the water rushing beneath me.

294. I love believing in miracles because that's the secret to making them happen.

295. I love FINDING things like coins on the ground and old letters in a drawer.

296. I love singing, especially when I know the lyrics.

297. I love watching swans floating on the water—they are so regal & beautiful!

298. I love seeing the way children bring out the "child" in their parents.

299. I love how I feel when I focus on the things that I love.

MARCH

300. I love getting good news, like not having to report for jury duty tomorrow.

301. I love LIGHT, but also the womb-like DARK out of which things are birthed.

302. I love getting to know people by learning what they love.

303. I love sitting in the garden on a sunny day reading a good book.

304. I love simple sayings that convey wisdom like "No Rain, No Rainbows."

305. I love NOT being shackled to a smart phone that I constantly monitor & monitors me.

306. I love wearing cargo pants with lots of pockets for all my stuff.

307. I love how creative we humans are with a deck of 52 cards!

308. I love the illustration of arrogance by the priest who said—"You go about God's work in your way, and I'll go about it in His."

309. I love how the ratio of unconscious to conscious bits of information we process is a trillion to one! Proof the world is MORE than we know.

310. I love bumping into just the right person who can help make my dream come true.

311. I love thinking about my Mom who recently passed away, especially today on her birthday.

312. I love watching flames dance on a candle or in a fireplace on a cold & cloudy day.

313. I love finding a piece of banana at the bottom of my smoothie, like a prize in a Cracker Jack box.

314. I love knowing when there's too much of a good thing—FIRE cooks but also burns, WATER quenches but also drowns!

315. I love weddings because everyone is so happy and filled with hope & love.

316. I love the paradox that giving is fulfilling, while withholding makes one feel empty.

You know quite well, deep within you, that there is only a single magic, a single power, a single salvation... and that is called loving.

— **Herman Hesse**

A Many-Splendored Thing

Science has discovered that love is more important to our health and wellbeing than previously imagined. Our entire biochemistry—even the DNA in our cells!—is profoundly affected by love.

We respond to love the way a plant responds to sunlight. Love, it turns out, is our essential nutrient. According to researcher Barbara Fredrickson, author of *Love 2.0*, "love is our supreme emotion. Its presence or absence in our lives influences everything we feel, think, do, and become."

More and more I was discovering that love is indeed "a many-splendored thing," and has a far greater impact on our lives than I ever realized.

APRIL

317. I love Fridays—it's like receiving a present, the weekend, I haven't unwrapped.

318. I love how much I've grown over the years.

319. I love my Mac, even when the beach ball of doom spins and it's on overload.

320. I love that no matter how "bad" things get, there are still things that I love in my life.

321. I love how clarifying it is to contemplate the question—What will you regret on your deathbed?

322. I love PROCESS—climbing the mountain more than standing at the top.

323. I love yoga and how the poses stretch the body and the mind.

324. I love this description of soulmates—one keeps the other grounded, while the other gives the one wings.

325. I love the irony of a couple walking down the street holding hands—each checking the phone in their free hand for messages!

326. I love how water—when it ripples on the surface of a pond—demonstrates how energy radiates all around us.

327. I love searching on Google for just the right image to illustrate a point.

328. I love the idea of a fast-food chain with treadmills that offers a discount to people who eat while walking on them.

329. I love watching sunsets, especially over a body of water.

330. I love remembering the times I've overcome adversity, especially today when I'm sick.

331. I love thinking about Joy, especially today on the 5th angel-versary of her passing.

332. On Good Friday I love thinking that life is a chain of "deaths" & "resurrections."

333. I love the feeling of being "guided" by loved ones on the "Other Side."

334. I love feeling better after I've been sick with a cold.

APRIL

335. I love dressing up in a formal tux, but only once in a while.

336. I love dancing to a live band, especially when the music has soul.

337. I love living where there are more trees than buildings, more green than grey.

338. I love revisiting precious moments I've captured on video.

339. I love how timing is everything—ripeness is all!

340. I love being able to wholeheartedly recommend someone's services—it's like gifting them & whoever might be looking for their help.

341. I love blowing dandelion seeds into the air, especially with children!

342. I love this Hawaiian word—humuhumunukunukuapua'a—and would love to learn what it means and how to pronounce it.

343. I love the art nature leaves behind in beautiful driftwood, rotting tree trunks & tangled vines.

344. I love when people volunteer to organize charity benefits that help others in need.

345. I love the idea of "pronoia"—the opposite of paranoia: the world isn't conspiring to harm, but rather to love me.

346. I love seeing ideas in my head fleshed out by a talented graphic designer.

347. I love feeling "at home" wherever I find myself.

348. I love helping someone feel good about themselves.

349. I love the idea of "karma"—that life's like a boomerang and you get back what you put out.

350. I love ice cream and that almost everyone else loves ice cream, too.

The hunger for love is much more
difficult to remove
than the hunger for bread.

— Mother Teresa

Vitamin L(ove) Deficiency

If love is an essential nutrient, we all suffer to one degree or another from a Vitamin Love deficiency. This is partly due to our innate survival instinct which focuses on and pays attention to what's *wrong* with a situation. This programming provided an evolutionary advantage—survival.

The media compounds the situation by manipulating our survival programming to focus on "what's wrong" in order to attract viewers, ratings and ultimately profits. Though there's lots of good news, we're bombarded with bad news by a media whose byword is: "If it bleeds, it leads!"

Now that I realized what an essential nutrient love is, I couldn't begin to imagine the consequences of Vitamin L deficiency on our health and happiness. What, I wondered, could be done about it?

APRIL

351. I love climbing up the library ladder into the loft—like having a tree house inside.

352. I love engaging with people—even in a doctor's office—in ways that bring out their humanity.

353. I love omelets with feta cheese and home fries in an old-fashioned diner.

354. I love the way "problems" sometimes magically work out.

355. I love roses—their color, fragrance, beauty & spiritual significance.

356. I love drum circles and how everyone beats the same rhythm, but has a different experience.

357. I love Native American ceremony—I don't know why but it always brings me to tears.

358. I love huddling in bed with my baby in the middle of the night as a storm thunders and flashes outside.

359. I love imagining living somewhere else more than actually moving.

360. I love learning that sperm has mental health benefits—"seminal fluid is a good anti-depressant, full of chemicals that lift optimism."

361. I love playing with my dog until he accidentally scratches me.

362. I love drawing pictures with a 3 year-old and being surprised by the results.

363. I love walking backwards uphill, exercising muscles I don't often use.

364. I love eating fruit and chocolate-filled crepe at a Sunday brunch.

365. I love walking a labyrinth on a full moon and receiving guidance.

366. I love visiting my parents' graves, especially with my one and only brother.

367. I love being astonished by people's amazing creativity.

APRIL

368. I love that the "story" of my life—how I interpret it—is up to me.

369. I love reclaiming my voice—finally speaking up about something that's been bothering me.

370. I love the avocado egg rolls at The Cheesecake Factory.

371. I love this wakeup call when I get lazy—"Wake up and smell the cemetery!"

372. I love the possibilities of forgiveness—forgiving others & being forgiven.

373. I love the insight that seeing my life from a "higher" perspective gives me.

374. I love to imagine "raindrop therapy"—that lying naked in the rain can cure illness.

375. I love living so that I'll have no regrets on my deathbed.

376. I love singing "oldies"—being surprised I know the words—& laughing my head off at how silly they were.

377. I love standing in the middle of a forest and being surrounded by Nature.

378. I love my geeky friends who can help me with computer problems.

379. I love the local "art cinema" where I can see quirky, independent movies.

380. I love reading something I wrote years ago and being surprised as if someone else had written it.

381. I love surfaces that reflect—glass, mirrors, water, polished metal.

382. I love it when talking about my past gives me new insight into that passage of my life.

383. I love seeing trees budding everywhere I look—it fills me with such anticipation.

384. I love visiting a tree nursery & meeting some adorable alpacas.

385. I love that—despite the common belief that "it's never as good as the 1st time"—so many things in my life get better & better.

Love is the great miracle cure.

Loving ourselves works miracles in our lives.

— Louise Hay

LoveRx
The Amazing Benefits of Vitamin L

I found research that demonstrated Vitamin L's amazing health and wellness benefits. Incredibly, love can heal as powerfully as medicine. *LoveRx!*

According to Dr. Eva Selhub of Harvard Medical School, "Love sets off a set of physiological events in the body: peptides and hormones are released, including endorphins, oxytocin, dopamine, vasopressin, and nitric oxide. These help turn off the fear response, evoke the relaxation response and create a positive physiology."

There's scientific evidence that Vitamin L can make you smarter, help fight cancer, as well as strengthen your immune, endocrine and cardiovascular systems. Vitamin L can lower your cholesterol as well as your blood pressure, reduce pain, and speed the healing of an injury. Sounded like a wonder drug!

Apparently, one of the greatest gifts I could give myself was a daily dose of Vitamin L.

APRIL

386. I love time-lapse photography that gives me a kind of God's POV.

387. I love how people, myself included, can turn an inherent weakness into a strength.

388. I love routine—so I can function on automatic pilot—and yet I love surprises.

389. I love sharing a hot tub with friends and seeing more of each other.

390. I love precious moments—like a red Cardinal singing 10 feet away.

391. I love accepting that for every "gift" I possess, I pay a "price" in another area of my life.

392. I love walking the dog or having the dog walk me, especially down an old country road.

393. I love making silly sounds in the morning with my love til we break up laughing.

394. I love noticing the beauty in people and telling them about it.

395. I love how adaptable I am, living in LI or LA, out of a suitcase if need be.

396. I love the excitement & reverence that surrounds the birth of a baby.

397. I love how a birth thins the veil between Here & the Hereafter.

398. I love holding a newborn and marveling at the miracle of life.

399. I love how a walk in nature refreshes me even if I'm exhausted.

400. I love witnessing a 90 year-old woman holding her day old great grandchild.

401. I love how the DVR enables me to enjoy my favorite shows when and how to the max.

402. I love having a great weekend weather forecast.

403. I love electricity, especially after an outage when the power comes back on.

APRIL

404. I love holding an infant and trying to imagine the adult it will become.

405. I love sleep-in Sundays—dream after dream after dream.

406. I love capturing precious moments on video like a mother and her newborn.

407. I love massaging my scalp while washing my hair in the shower.

408. I love "making lemonade out of lemons," even having a lemonade stand.

409. I love the idea that orgasm promotes health and prevents disease.

410. I love a new toothbrush that gives my gums a workout.

411. I love having a dream I can bring into reality.

412. I love the idea that, in the same way we swaddle infants to make them feel safe, religion swaddles adults.

413. I love the convenience of ordering Chinese food that's delivered to my home after a long, tiring day.

414. I love the way loving someone inspires people's creativity.

415. I love hearing jokes that tickle my funny bone and make me laugh til it hurts.

416. I love blowing kisses back & forth with a 3 year-old.

417. I love conversations that remind me of something important I've forgotten.

418. I love walking thru a fog down to the water's edge and smelling the salty sea.

419. I love visiting a museum where I can see how other artists have been visited by their muse.

420. I love thinking of my father & his enigmatic expression "If you knew what I know," and only now beginning to understand what he was saying.

Water is the driving force in nature.

— Leonardo da Vinci

Liquid Love

Dr. Masaru Emoto's groundbreaking book, *Messages from Water,* helped me understand how love could have such a profound effect. He used powerful electron microscopes to capture newly formed crystals in frozen water samples and discovered that *water reacts to our thoughts, words and emotions.*

According to Dr. Emoto, water exposed to loving words showed brilliant, complex, and beautiful crystals. In contrast, water influenced by negative thoughts or words formed incomplete, asymmetrical, ugly crystals. The most beautiful crystals, Dr. Emoto said, were formed when they were exposed to the words or emotion of *Love.*

The human body is more than 60% water. Our blood is 92%, our brain and muscles are 75%, and even our bones are about 22% water. Whenever we think about what we love, the water in us experiences this magical effect.

MAY

421. I love meeting someone who opens up a whole new world for me to explore.

422. I love when the sun comes out, especially after days of clouds and rain.

423. I love a play-on-words, like the t-shirts at the seafood joint that say "Lobstertrician."

424. I love asking someone what they would do if money were no object & they were financially independent?

425. I love how bouncing on my trampoline moves the lymphatic ocean in my body.

426. I love walking in moss-carpeted woods where I hear the honk of a bullfrog.

427. I love the way the light changes throughout the day from dawn to dusk.

428. I love being transported by a kiss.

429. I love sitting under a tree watching a Blue Jay and hearing a Cardinal.

430. I love reading journal entries from years ago and being reminded of things I'd forgotten.

431. I love the Sufi mystic Rumi & how his almost 1000 yr old poetry speaks to me.

432. I love asking someone the right question that, like a key, opens the door to intimacy.

433. I love the fragrance of a peony flower.

434. I love mirroring clarity back to a confused friend who's trying to make a decision.

435. I love being able to stop my mail when I go away and picking it up when I return.

436. I love being able to fly thousands of miles to be with those I love.

437. I love how a good night's sleep renews me and how a good dream inspires me.

438. I love thinking that whatever broke my heart will become a "gift" that ultimately expands it.

MAY

439. I love hearing bird song, cricket choirs and whale symphonies.

440. I love completing things because it's so much harder than starting them.

441. I love my body's capacity to heal itself.

442. I love contemplating the Mystery of the Orgasm—and researching it, too!

443. I love dry, clear days when you can see for miles.

444. I love meeting older people who are more vibrant and alive than ever.

445. I love feeling that I'm fulfilling my life's purpose.

446. I love appreciating something about the people I meet as I go about my day.

447. I love that we're creatures of habit—especially the good ones.

448. I love working hard for something I love.

449. I love when people blow out the candles on their birthday cake.

450. I love that the word "enthusiasm" means to be filled with the divine spirit.

451. I love the cries of unbridled exhilaration you hear at an amusement park.

452. I love watercolors, especially knowing how difficult they are to do.

453. I love how we dance with the paradox that Death is inevitable yet inconceivable.

454. I love how wordplay reveals the word "love" mirrored in the first 4 letters of "evolution."

455. I love those meditations when just breathing is so delicious, it's enough!

456. I love how quickly I recovered my bearings after a recent career disappointment.

457. I love when a Sunday is a sunny day!

Something amazing happens

when we surrender and just love.

We melt into another world,

a realm of power already within us.

The world changes when we change.

the world softens when we soften.

The world loves us when we choose to love the world.

— Marianne Williamson

Love—Our Untapped Resource

Despite the media's daily drumbeat of "the sky is falling" headlines, studies show that people experience far more good than bad in their lives. Statistically, for every negative experience, we'll have three or more positive ones. The fact is that most of us live in a relatively safe world, and experience an abundance of good versus bad.

Unfortunately, we are at the mercy of our instinctual survival programming. We pay attention to the bad in our lives while often being indifferent to the good. Perhaps a key to transforming our lives is to simply pay attention to what we love.

I began to see love as an untapped resource. When we cast a *LoveSpell*, we "mine" our lives for the "gold" of what we love and become physically and emotionally enriched. Fortified by our growing awareness of all that we love, we're better able to deal with adversity when it inevitably arrives.

MAY

458. I love mornings like today when I'm awakened by birdsong instead of my alarm clock.

459. I love exploring the impossibility of complete stillness—my heart beats, my blood flows, my cells divide—I metabolize!

460. I love doing 7 yoga sun salutations as a thank you for my health, strength, endurance, agility, well-being, body & life.

461. I love looking for & finding the "gifts" of my retinal problems & not seeing well—for example: how young my TweetHeart looks.

462. I love that when I laugh, hope, try, hurt, fear & cry, I'm just like everyone else.

463. I love eating in a restaurant that puts rolls of paper towels on the table as "napkins."

464. I love sitting in a limo once in a while & seeing that's it's no big deal.

465. I love rough washcloths and soft towels.

466. I love knowing that often the difference between a "medicine" & a "poison" is the dose.

467. I love putting quotes around ideas like "success" & "failure," "good" & "bad."

468. I love wondering how much of who I am is a result of nature or nurture or chance?

469. I love having a passion—it's so much sexier than having a hobby.

470. I love how on our walks my dog sniffs what I can't see reminding me how much of the world is invisible to our senses.

471. I love the irony that the most exciting tech word for innovation is "disruption"

472. I love passing a fragrant wisteria vine on my daily walk.

473. I love wondering if the ultimate cost of machines that think is people who don't?

474. I love having a day off after what seems like a solid week of non-stop activity.

MAY

475. I love when a hurtful breakdown in communication becomes a breakthrough that enhances the relationship

476. I love wondering what it would be like to be a leaf at the top of a tall tree?

477. I love how important smiling is to us—studies say we regularly use over 50 different kinds of smiles.

478. I love reminding someone who has difficulty saying NO to other people how healthy it is to say YES to oneself.

479. I love those times when a song, a painting, a moment—gives me the chills.

480. I love how for a toddler an empty toilet paper roll becomes a magical telescope.

481. I love wondering if todays grand project of the INTERNET is our TOWER OF BABEL?

482. I love Oscar Wilde's quip re: nudity—"If god had intended me to be nude, I'd have been born that way."

483. I love the way music invites memories—it's really time-travel!

484. I love visiting the home & studio of a still productive 90 yr old sculptress.

485. I love the comical catch-22 my TweetHeart revealed when she confided "I love burnt food but I'm afraid of fire."

486. I love that we're all born with unique gifts—as a great basketball coach once said, "You can't teach height!"

487. I love petting my dog and knowing it's good for both of us.

488. I love ironies, even hypothetical ones—like the study of happiness causing depression.

489. I love the conversation that follows when you ask a couple which one of them is happier?

490. I love the orgasm of flowers blooming—Nature's porn!

Only one thing has to change

for us to know happiness in our lives:

where we focus our attention.

— **Greg Anderson**

Triple AAA-ing My Life

Neuroscience has discovered that paying close attention to anything increases our enjoyment of it. Unfortunately, we often overlook moments that could delight us.

The Washington Post conducted a social experiment that demonstrated this. They asked a world-famous violinist to give a concert in a Washington D.C. subway station during rush hour. Thousands of commuters passed what appeared to be just another street musician, but only seven stopped to listen.

How many delights do we miss because we're not paying attention? Studies have shown that adopting strategies which help us pay attention, also helps us find delight where before we were indifferent.

In his utopian novel, *The Island*, Aldous Huxley imagined an enlightened society on a tropical island that trained its parrots to squawk, *Pay Attention!*

My *LoveSpell Experiment* required that I pay attention and savor the beauty, joy and pleasure in my life. By *Acknowledging, Appreciating* and paying *Attention* to what I love, I was *Triple AAA-ing* my life.

MAY

491. I love learning what our technology does TO us as well as FOR us.

492. I love talking to my dog and to babies in their language—it takes me out of my mind and into the meaning of pure sound.

493. I love that 99% of the atoms in our bodies are replaced in the course of a year.

494. I love my TweetHeart's love of flowers—it adds color to my life.

495. I love being aware that we get used to positive circumstances—to things that feel good—so things that once thrilled us no longer do.

496. I love that as I get older, I'm less interested in the WHAT of the things I do & more interested in the HOW, and even more, the WHY!

497. I love toning, humming even singing—it feels like an inner massage.

498. I love the symbolism in the sun being always the same and the moon always changing.

499. I love creating order & organization on my computer's desktop—why don't I do it more often?

500. I love being rescued by a Good Samaritan—especially when I've locked myself out of my home.

501. I love knowing that Happiness isn't about getting something I DON'T have, but recognizing & appreciating what I DO have.

502. I love that my TweetHeart and I hug a lot—every day and throughout the day.

503. Once in awhile I love pigging out on pretzels, M&Ms & chocolate!

504. I love walking through a bamboo forest.

505. I love the irony that the idea of "Heaven" is hell because "Heaven" has so much judgment associated with it.

506. I love the common-sense advice "Never ask a barber if you need a haircut."

MAY

507. I love remembering to appreciate my food & to chew it well.

508. I love having a great handyman who can do all the things I don't love to do.

509. I love drinking wine over dinner & toasting & the more we drink, the more we toast!

510. I love having sacrificed for someone I love.

511. I love those moments with my dog when I wonder who is training who?

512. I love having banished "if only" from my thinking.

513. I love teaching people about HUGS—the difference between left & right-sided hugs when you're heart to heart.

514. I love watching a squirrel trying to figure out a supposedly squirrel-proof bird feeder.

515. I love that programming computers to be funny is the last frontier—humor doesn't translate into 1s & 0s.

516. I love looking up at the stars on a clear night and being awed like I was as a child.

517. I love knowing my limits—to compassion, to distraction, to self-absorption.

518. I love the idea that each of us has a PASSWORD FOR LIFE—for some it's FREEDOM, for others it's PLAY, for many it's MONEY and for others it's HOPE or JOY.

519. I love celebrating Memorial Day Weekend & the unofficial start of summer with a BBQ.

520. I love hearing a young couple exchange intimate & heartfelt vows at their wedding ceremony.

521. I love how a funeral—especially standing graveside—inspires me to live more fully.

522. I love that the human brain has 85-100 billion neurons—the same amount as the stars in the galaxy or the galaxies in the universe.

Love is the master key

which opens the gates of happiness.

— Oliver Wendell Holmes

The LoveSpell Secret

From both my research and my experience *beating the drum for love*, I realized that Joy's New Year's Eve question—*What do you love?*—had shown me how to open the treasure chest of my life.

My daily declarations of love created a magical spell—a quantum *LoveSpell*—that expanded the love in my life. With Joy's help I'd stumbled upon one of the secrets to happiness—the *LoveSpell Secret*.

The message of religion, philosophy and countless pop songs boils down to a simple truth—*Love is the Answer*. For many people, that simplistic idea is a sentimental cliché. But like some fairy tale, the real secret is hidden within an Alice-in-Wonderland-like paradox.

Love is indeed the Answer. But that's only partly true. By taking the cliché, *"Love is the Answer."* and turning it around so that *"Love is the Question,"* I had discovered the *LoveSpell Secret*—a magical key to transform my life.

JUNE

523. I love cleverness and wit, especially when it's not mean-spirited.

524. I love almonds, blueberries, cherries, dates, eggs, figs & grapefruit...

525. I love hummus, ice cream, jam, kidney beans, lentils, mushrooms, nuts...

526. I love olives, pineapple, quiche, raisins, strawberries, tomatoes, walnuts, wine, yogurt & yams.

527. I love the spiral shape, from small seashells to large galaxies.

528. I love lying on my couch and losing myself in a good movie.

529. I love cheesecake—I can't help myself.

530. I love being turned on to good music, especially if I can dance to it.

531. I love finding new reasons to celebrate.

532. I love clever book titles like "Drinking Problems At The Fountain of Youth."

533. I love the cycles of life—there's a time and a season for everything.

534. I love the irony that sex—i.e. pornography—has been the chief driver of technological innovation from the VCR to the Internet.

535. I love when people whistle—it's usually a sign they're in a good mood.

536. I love the synergy between the words "trust" and "hope."

537. I love talking to teenagers who are excited about their lives.

538. I love the cooing of pigeons and the chirping of crickets.

539. I love the unusual, and yet I'm comforted by the familiar.

540. I love Bonobo monkeys because they resolve conflicts with sex not aggression.

541. I love the weekend because it's pregnant with possibility.

JUNE

542. I love the way schools of fish and flocks of birds move together as one.

543. I love kaleidoscopes and their ever-changing hypnotic beauty.

544. I love how playing with children gives me permission to "make believe."

545. I love how real dreams can feel and how dream-like reality can be.

546. I love how the moon waxes & wanes and goes from new to full every 28 days.

547. I love when people donate their time & money to a worthy cause.

548. I love butterflies—as things of beauty and symbols of transformation.

549. I love working with someone on a project—collaboration is the coolest!

550. I love losing myself with an infant, preferably when they're not crying!

551. I love how relationships—platonic & erotic—add new dimensions to my life.

552. I love when meltdowns and breakdowns turn into breakthroughs.

553. I love being able to take care of a sick friend.

554. I love turning a calamity into an opportunity—seeing how the "curse" could possibly be a blessing.

555. I love watching the sun set into the sea—glup, glup, glup

556. I love coming up with questions that help people get to know themselves.

557. I love the word TRUST—it's one of the keys to HAPPINESS!

558. I love meeting eccentric people and hearing about their lives.

559. I love getting giddy—it doesn't matter why—and laughing at everything!

Your habits become your values,

Your values become your destiny.

— Mahatma Gandhi

The Love Body

In her book, *Love For No Reason*, Marci Shimoff talks about the "love-body." She compares it to the "pain-body" Eckhart Tolle described in his bestselling book, *The Power of Now.*

According to Tolle, the pain-body is comprised of all the painful emotions and memories we carry around with us. It's easily triggered by negative thoughts and experiences. Since the pain-body feeds on pain, it's always looking for opportunities to experience worry, conflict, dissatisfaction and negativity of any sort. In short, it filters for what's *wrong*. Most of us are in the habit of feeding our pain-body.

Shimoff theorizes that "If there's a pain-body that magnetizes pain to you, there must also be a love-body that magnetizes love to you!"

My *LoveSpell Experiment* proves her theory. Answering Joy's question—*What do I love?*—created a new habit of filtering for what's *right*. By doing so, I was feeding my love-body. And attracting more love into my life.

JUNE

560. I love my TweetHeart's optimism—misreading the word Optometrist as "Open to Trust"—talk about seeing what you want to see!

561. I love the quiet before the storm of lawn mowers, leaf blowers & weed whackers drown out the birdsong.

562. I love that my TweetHeart and I share the same date but different months for our birthdays—the 12th.

563. I love that my self worth is not a function of my net worth—but $ doesn't hurt.

564. I love the idea that REALITY is a striptease of layers of illusion—REALITEASE!

565. I love walking in the woods and imagining living in another era.

566. I love to be reminded that "Someday" is NOT one of the days of the week so that I realize my goals & dreams.

567. I love finding imaginative ways to ask people "What's your Yes?"

568. I love when serendipity occurs & suddenly life seems to be the result of the most amazing plan!

569. I love doing radio interviews to share my incredible experiences & what I've learned from them.

570. I love catching a wave & body surfing all the way to shore.

571. I love finally realizing that no matter what new thing thrills us—we go from novel to normal to numb.

572. I love staring into the eyes of a 3-month old as if into a mirror, wondering what it was like NOT to be distracted by my thoughts.

573. I love taking a Sab-bath with my TweetHeart—floating out of the scattered day-to-day into our w-holiness.

JUNE

574. I love when my hammock swings so low to the ground that blades of grass tickle my back—it's Zen-sational!

575. I love remembering those times I've been so aligned I could almost read the secret language embossed on the bark of a tree.

576. I love laughing my head off in a doctor's examining room trying to hum the song "Tomorrow" from Annie.

577. I love how creative I become when I have to soothe an unhappy toddler.

578. I love introducing my TweetHeart as my Emergency Contact.

579. I love that every day we pass some point-of-no-return about something in our lives.

580. I love remembering great sex: in the ocean, on the hood of a car outside a bar, and on a swinging bed.

581. I love sitting at the ocean's edge letting the surf toss me here & there—SURRENDER!

582. I love waking my TweetHeart from a nightmare, then making love to soothe her.

583. I love Hinduism's belief that everything in the universe is connected in a vast web called "Indra's Net." Sound familiar?

584. I love when an argument ends with some new insight into the underlying reasons for it that enhances the relationship.

585. I love the irony that two substances made of almost identical carbon atoms—graphite & diamonds—are the softest & hardest solids.

586. I love being reminded by the ocean that our lives are like the waves—briefly rising then falling back into the primordial sea.

587. I love glue—real or metaphorical—& how it helps us mend what's broken in our lives.

588. I love thinking of the imagination as a bridge across which we reach for the infinite & the infinite reaches for us.

You don't want a million answers

as much as you want a few forever questions.

— Richard Bach

The Question Determines the Quest

Questions are the key.

It's no accident that the word "quest" derives from the word "question." Our lives are a result of asking questions that propel us on quests to answer them. The question you ask determines the quest you take.

When you think of a *quest*, you probably think of the *Knights of the Round Table*. In myth we slay dragons; in reality, we pose and answer questions. Understanding that the power of search is based on questions, reinforced the idea that *asking the right questions* is a key to living a fulfilling life.

What do I love? is one of the most important questions you can ask. The more you answer that question, the more love you will discover on your life's quest.

JUNE

589. I love celebrating the summer solstice and appreciating how the sun is the source of EVERYTHING.

590. I love dancing with my shadow in the moonlight.

591. I love immersing myself so deeply in the woods that I begin to feel like a tree.

592. I love the way moss looks & feels in the dappled sunlight of a forest.

593. I love seeing fireflies flash on and off at dusk.

594. I love the rumble of thunder more than the flash of lightning.

595. I love it when someone's love overcomes their fear and they act.

596. I love inexplicable archaeological anomalies that suggest humanity is much older than we realize.

597. I love seeing a spider's web sparkling like diamonds with morning dew.

598. I love how my TweetHeart put herself to sleep last night by declaring all the things she loves.

599. I love hearing about someone's miraculous experience.

600. I love getting good news, especially when it's unexpected.

601. I love finding money—pennies in the street or checks in the mail.

602. I love throwing a metaphorical rope to someone who's fallen into an emotional pit.

603. I love the quiet after a crying infant falls asleep.

604. I love lighthouses—as a metaphor and as an exotic fantasy place to live.

605. I love red pens for editing things I've written.

606. I love being able to step onto an empty dance floor to "warm it up" so that people feel it's safe to get up & dance.

JUNE

607. I love spending time with horses—they're so gentle and yet so powerful.

608. I love the way life unfolds—more surprising than anything I can plan.

609. I love snuggling in bed during an afternoon thunderstorm.

610. I love finding solutions to problems, answers to questions, and keys to locks.

611. I love taking a break, especially when I'm frustrated and feel like I'm stuck.

612. I love going to the beach on a hot summer day!

613. I love salmon cooked so it's moist, pasta so it's chewy and chocolate any old way.

614. I love watching people playing catch with a ball—especially a man and woman.

615. I love auspicious days like today—a birthday, an anniversary and a full moon!

616. I love the sudden downpour at the beach when kids in bathing suits danced wildly in the rain.

617. I love how the internet makes researching a subject so easy.

618. I love how declaring what I love is just another way to practice gratitude.

619. I love when adults confess to their parents all their childhood misbehavior, and everyone laughs about it.

620. I love how some people can use a pendulum to get guidance.

621. I love the long days of summer—light & life at its fullest.

622. I love eating a ripe peach that's so juicy it runs down my chin.

623. I love walking in a summer rain, especially since I don't have them in LA.

624. I love sitting quietly in the garden until I can perceive how busy it actually is.

We are shaped and fashioned by what we love.

— Goethe

Google Myself

In our Digital Age, we've come to understand the power of *search*. Every day we search for answers. Searches are driven by questions.

By repeatedly asking myself Joy's question *What do I love?*, I'd in effect typed a search term into my consciousness. I'd googled myself. After a few months, I had programmed myself to automatically scan my life throughout the day for things that I loved.

What do I love? became a background mantra to my thoughts. Wherever I was, whatever I was doing, I asked myself—*What do I love here? What do I love about this?* And by simply asking the question, I received an answer.

JULY

625. I love visiting summer camp, especially since I didn't go as a child.

626. I love Indian teepees painted with beautiful designs.

627. I love learning to hit a golf ball at a driving range.

628. I love swimming so much my shoulders ache the next day.

629. I love being in the country & walking through the woods along an old Indian trail.

630. I love the fatigue that comes from physical activity—swimming, hiking, etc.

631. I love driving in the carpool lane, especially in traffic.

632. I love publishing a new book♥ that helps parents grieving the loss of a child.

♥ Lilly helped me adapt my book, *Grief Quest*, for parents who've lost a child. *Grief Quest: A Workbook & Journal to Heal the Grieving Parent's Heart*

633. I love learning to square dance and laughing at how badly I do.

634. I love licking ice cream from a cone, especially on a hot summer day.

635. I love thinking that I'm like a prism refracting the light/life-force of the sun into a rainbow that is my life.

636. I love cooling off in the ocean on a hot summer day.

637. I love GPS navigation, even though it sometimes screws up.

638. I love watching butterflies, usually in pairs, flitting around the garden.

639. I love wondering what new religion will free us from the tyranny of the old one?

640. I love getting stuff done, almost as much as I love doing nothing.

641. I love when I act heroically in my dreams—when I'm compassionate & loving rather than fearful & defensive.

JULY

642. I love it when a child beats me at putting together a jigsaw puzzle.

643. I love driving on a gently rolling tree-lined country road.

644. I love being reminded of wonderful experiences that I'd forgotten.

645. I love ice cream—I may be an ice cream-aholic. Ice cream-anon?

646. I love when a little girl announces—"Today I'm going to face my fears!"

647. I love creating a meal out of all the leftovers in the fridge.

648. I love seeing a rainbow on the 4th of July, even before all the fireworks!

649. I love imagining a society where people are encouraged not just to pursue happiness but to achieve their unique fulfillment.

650. I love coming home to LA even though I feel at home in LI.

651. I love lying on my hammock and feeling raindrops fall from the sky, giggling helplessly as if God was tickling me.

652. I love wondering what it's like for someone who uses chopsticks to eat with a fork for the 1st time.

653. I love when I let go of my agenda and things work out better than I planned.

654. I love teaching people how to hug, especially those who are grieving the loss of their child.♥

655. I love hearing about people who blossom through adversity.

656. I love "vegging" in front of the TV after a busy, stressful week.

657. I love that I didn't know THEN what I know NOW, cuz THEN wouldn't have been THEN.

♥ After reading the *Journey of a Thousand Hugs* chapter in my memoir, Lilly suggested my experience could be adapted to help parents who'd lost a child. Together we developed the *Healing Touch For Grieving Couples* workshop that we presented at the national conference of the Compassionate Friends.

There is nothing either good or bad,

but thinking makes it so.

— Shakespeare

Filters

We all have filters through which we view the world that translate our experience and give it meaning. They filter our experience in ways unique to us. We see what has meaning for us.

Too often, our filters (products of our upbringing, culture or religion) are some variation of what's *wrong* as opposed to what's *right*. Some of us walk around all day filtering for "I don't like this..." Others filter for "This isn't fair" or "Why do they always...?"

Though we all have them, we're often unaware of our own filters. But we can clearly see the filters of those around us—friends who filter for "Why does this always happen to me," or family members who view the world through "the glass-is-half-empty" filters.

Few of us were taught as children to filter for what's *right* in our world. It requires creating a new search filter to perceive a new reality. Creating a new habit of searching for things we love changes our perception of the world.

Joy's question had prompted me to create a filter for love. I began to see new loves in old familiar routines and unexpected places. I began viewing my world through "love-colored glasses," and realized that my previous world had been a pale version of the vibrant aliveness I now experienced.

JULY

658. I love to see babies laugh (on average 300 times/day while adults laugh only 10 times/ day).

659. I love taking a deep breath, especially after seeing my credit card bill.

660. I love getting a "sandwich kiss"—giving it is pretty good, too.

661. I love the idea of putting the "fun" back in funerals.

662. I love the sound of a ball hitting the bat just right.

663. I love the irony that the most important things in life often happen because we DIDN'T get what we thought we wanted.

664. I love making my TweetHeart happy!

665. I love watching butterflies & hummingbirds breakfasting in the garden.

666. I love showering someone I love with appreciations.

667. I love candlelight—it flickers and dances and casts a magical spell.

668. I love being efficient—filling the car with gas and buying flowers at the same time.

669. I love walking along the beach, especially a nude beach.

670. I love checking off my To Do List—it gives me a sense of accomplishment.

671. I love it when I'm adaptable, flexible and go with the flow.

672. I love standing in a summer rain—the original shower.

673. I love the sensation of a cool ocean breeze, especially on a hot day.

674. I love afternoon naps, especially on the weekend.

675. I love air-conditioning—especially during this 100+ degree heat spell.

JULY

676. I love finding a better feeling—that's the secret to navigating the bends, turns and pitfalls of life.

677. I love dreaming, both the day kind and the night kind.

678. I love bananas—especially in my morning smoothie.

679. I love that there are infinite points of view so life is never boring.

680. I love the ever-changing beauty that clouds continually display.

681. I love having hot & cold running water 24/7—what a luxury!

682. I love when a friend calls out of the blue and says "I miss you!"

683. I love hearing other people's love stories, especially since I've lived one of the greatest!

684. I love "straightening up" and "getting organized" once in awhile.

685. I love Gravity because it keeps me (and everything else) grounded.

686. I love rubber bands, paper clips, staples, post-its and highlighters!

687. I love that it's our position relative to the millstone of life's travails—our attitude—that determines whether we're ground to dust or polished into a diamond.

688. I love crunchy salads filled with cucumbers, tomatoes, sugar snap peas and walnuts.

689. I love NOT being tethered to a smart phone—don't know how much longer I can hold out.

690. I love walking barefoot in grass still wet with morning dew.

691. I love a good sandwich for lunch.

692. I love listening to the symphony of cicadas on a summer night.

693. I love discovering new ways to have FUN!

A World of Love

As friends and family became aware of my *LoveSpell Experiment*, they wanted to play the game, too. So I asked them what they loved. Not *who*, but *what do you love?*

Here's a sampling of other people's loves:

- *I love making a perfect tuna fish salad.*
- *I love to clean my house.*
- *I love eating a hot dog with all the fixin's at a baseball game.*
- *I love to catch the lights when I drive down 2nd Avenue in Manhattan.*
- *I love folding laundry.*
- *I love to play in the garden and feel the earth with my fingers.*
- *I love finding a new use for an old thing.*
- *I love feeling the tug of a fish on the end of my line.*
- *I love to rollerblade along the boardwalk.*
- *I love fixing things.*
- *I love singing in a choir.*
- *I love playing golf on a beautiful course.*
- *I love going to Vegas!*
- *I love shopping, especially finding bargains!*

- *I love hopping on my motorcycle and riding like the wind!*
- *I love NASCAR...the faster & louder the better!*
- *I love my glue gun!*
- *I love basketball, baseball, football...any kind of ball!*
- *I love playing poker! And winning!*
- *I love money—making it, counting it, investing it, growing it!*

The world is full of things to love. Each of our lives is filled with things we love. When we become aware of our loves, we magnify our enjoyment and their *LoveRx* benefits.

Every single one of us can do things
that no one else can do,
can love things
that on one else can love.

— Barbara Sher

JULY

694. I love discovering new ways to play and then passing them on.

695. I love solitude, yet I don't feel lonely.

696. I love the idea that our favorite children's stories imprint us for the rest of our lives.

697. I love thanking people & appreciating them.

698. I love good lighting—for mood and for reading.

699. I love watching someone get up after they've fallen down—call it a comeback or a redemption.

700. I love thinking about someone and then they call me "out of the blue."

701. I love hearing about people's NDEs (near-death experience) and their adventures on the Other Side.

702. I love my selective memory—remembering some delightful ones and forgetting painful others.

703. Now that I'm older, I love helping people more than entertaining them.

704. I love these things about TIME—anticipating & remembering.

705. I love feeling that my life has purpose.

706. I love the Greek story of Lysistrata—about women withholding sex to stop a war.

707. I love the "miracles" that never-giving-up can produce.

708. I love veils—they're mysterious & sexy.

709. I love new ideas that can be like filters through which I see a new world.

710. I love how you can learn about somebody by the way they load a dishwasher.

711. I love laughing at myself, more than having people laugh at me.

712. I love trading in my wit for wonder—I'd rather be awestruck than funny.

JULY

713. I love being hungry—it makes everything taste so good!

714. I love learning from animals—for example, how geese fly in formation to give each other lift.

715. I love loving different things now than what I loved as a young man, a teenager, a child.

716. I love viewing politics—especially the presidential campaign—as an Olympic competition in hypocrisy.

717. I love that it's not lifting weights that makes me stronger, it's lifting myself up when I'm knocked down.

718. I love finding stuff in storage I once cherished—even though now it's dusty.

719. I love the notion that the world is divided into two types of people: those who fold and those who crumple their toilet paper.

720. I love how animals can do things humans can't like bloodhounds smelling time.

721. I love nail clippers—they're genius!

722. I love to catch myself playing the "blame game"—then shifting from "victim" to "victor" to take back my power.

723. I love being inspired by animals—the two cormorants, each with one wing, who hang out together and won't quit.

724. I love "forest bathing"—everywhere I look I see a mirror of myself: trees are my lungs, vines are my veins, the stream is my blood.

725. I love the lesson I learned at the Butterfly Farm—the struggle to break out of the cocoon is what fills the butterfly's wings.

726. I love helping someone who's grieving the loss of a loved one by sharing my experience with grief.

727. I love WD-40 because it makes everything it touches slippery & quiet.

728. I love napping by the pool in the afternoon as a gentle sea breeze caresses my body.

The privilege of a lifetime

is to become who you truly are.

— Carl Jung

Loving Your Way To A Fulfilled Life

A nurse who spent years caring for the terminally ill during the last weeks of their life learned about their most common regrets. She discovered that the number one regret of people who were dying was wishing they'd had the courage to live a life true to themselves, not the life others expected of them.

Too many of us spend our lives trying to please others, and so never really discover who we truly are and what we really love. We miss the opportunity to live a life that truly expresses our unique individuality.

I couldn't help but wonder if the *LoveSpell Secret* was an antidote to that common deathbed regret? Could asking and answering the simple question *What do I love?* help us live a life that embodies our values and is truly fulfilling? Perhaps yet another benefit of embarking on a *LoveSpell Experiment* is loving your way to a fulfilled life.

AUGUST

729. I love walking barefoot on the beach—my feet receiving a reflexology massage from the sand.

730. I love that when I was young I often felt looked at by life, but as I got older the more of life I looked at and saw.

731. I love saying "I could be wrong"—it feels so right!

732. I love when people see that the "blessings" of past relationships come in many different ways.

733. I love finding beautiful seashells on the shore even though I don't know what to do with them.

734. I love looking deeply into someone eyes, especially if they're open to In-To-Me-See.

735. I love how after sex people used to reach for a cigarette, but now they reach for their smartphone & check messages.

736. I love spinning like a whirling dervish on the beach until I lose my sense of self.

737. I love imagining my commencement speech—Your success won't be won by the answers you've learned, but by the questions you've learned to ask.

738. I love how our bodies are our last refuge in Nature as we become increasingly lost in the hall of mirrors created by our minds.

739. I love realizing that religion is the ultimate placebo—effective if you believe in it.

740. I love watching my TweetHeart teach her 4 yr old granddaughter how to bake bread.

741. I love the irony that parents concerned about their kids' addiction to screens have taken pictures of every moment of their lives.

742. I love how often we tell stories about the terrible things that have happened to us which now make us laugh.
Tragedy + Time = Comedy.

743. I love the triumph I experience every morning when I conquer my laziness by doing yoga.

AUGUST

744. I love waking up and thinking, "Today I'm going to camp!"♥

745. I love playing *Trading Secrets*♥♥ on a 4 hour road trip and getting to know everyone (including myself) better.

746. I love being in the mountains where I can see the stars so clearly at night.

747. I love being so hungry that even camp food tastes delicious.

748. I love shooting hoops, especially when the basketball goes SWISH.

749. I love playing ping-pong & eating ice cream sandwiches at the camp canteen.

750. I love silly games like who can empty a tissue box—one tissue at a time—the fastest.

♥ Lilly's grief organization COPE was sponsoring Camp Erin, NYC—a weekend bereavement camp in the Poconos for children ages 6-17 who had lost a parent or sibling. This was the inaugural year and we were going up to volunteer.

♥♥ Joy created *Trading Secrets*—a deck of thought-provoking questions to stimulate conversation and help people get to know themselves and each other.

751. I love sitting by a bonfire, roasting Smores and getting sleepy.

752. I love hearing a child say—"My parents are so poor they have to share the same bed."

753. I love competing in a bucket brigade contest and winning.

754. I love lighting a luminary candle for my departed loved ones and setting it adrift on a moonlit lake.

755. I love experiencing firsts like "tubing"—being towed by a motorboat on a lake.

756. I love the story about a child who said—"My Daddy must be Superman because he puts his fist through walls."

757. I love being part of a healing weekend for children who are grieving the loss of a parent or sibling.

758. I love seeing deer in the woods—a mother and her fawn staring back at me.

Love doesn't just sit there, like a stone.

It has to be made, like bread;

re-made all the time, made new.

— Ursula LeGuin

Strengthening My Love Muscle

Casting a *LoveSpell* for the entire year wasn't going to be easy. When I did something new and exciting—visiting a summer camp or leading a workshop at a bereavement conference—it wasn't hard to find things to love. But finding new things to love in my daily routine was much more difficult.

What can I love about shopping for food, waiting in line at the post office, driving in traffic? How about getting up in the morning and going to bed at night? Eating? Sleeping? Even breathing?

I saw the progression. First, declaring the easy loves. Then hunting for the boring, routine things to love. And finally, finding something to love in difficult situations and circumstances

What could I find to love in career disappointments and setbacks? Financial pressures? Personal conflicts? Even illness?

If I was going to fulfill my New Year's Resolution, I'd have to progress from beginner to intermediate to advanced *lover*. Loving more and more of my life would ultimately require mastery.

I hoped that my daily workout of casting a *LoveSpell* was strengthening my *LoveMuscle* so that one day I could love even the "unlovable" parts of my life. What a gift that would be!

AUGUST

759. I love swinging in the hammock with my TweetHeart until we're both fast asleep.

760. I love spending time with the people whom I share history, yet I also love getting to know a stranger.

761. I love running jokes, sometimes too much—I'm like a dog with a bone who won't let go.

762. I love the paradox that doing nothing and doing it well, takes lots of practice.

763. I love that when someone doesn't like me, I can practice not taking it personally—what they think of me is their problem!

764. I love the irony when a person complains that people repeat themselves, but doesn't realize it's because they're not listening!

765. I love the girl at camp who was thoughtful enough to bring earplugs for her bunkmates so they wouldn't be bothered by her snoring.

766. I love seeing a boat docked in the Marina named "Therapy."

767. I love the undeniably positive-thinking of the t-shirt that said—"I'll make better mistakes tomorrow!"

768. I love going on a road trip whose destination is Nice People Place. Look it up in your GPS!

769. I love shooting baskets even in flipflops and finally swishing three jumpers in a row.

770. I love skipping a stone over the mirror-like surface of a lake that ripples the reflections.

771. I love the paradox that any key that opens Heaven's Gate also opens the Gates of Hell. Try the INTERNET Key. Or the IMAGINATION Key. Or the SEX Key & see!

772. I love listening to a bluegrass festival in a park by the beach on a beautiful day.

773. I love finally overcoming my procrastination about something I've been wanting to do but haven't done.

AUGUST

774. I love filming meditations of Nature, especially around water—lakes, streams, surf.

775. I love Plato's observation—"You can discover more about a person in an hour of play than in a year of conversation."

776. I love playing with a yo-yo—it reminds me of being a carefree child.

777. I love overhead fans on hot days, especially when they're quiet.

778. I love hearing from a stranger that something I've written made a difference in their life.

779. I love recording "firsts" on video so they can be savored again & again.

780. I love leftovers—I'm not sure if it's because there's no preparation or if it actually tastes better.

781. I love telling a child a bedtime story that puts me to sleep.

782. I love crystal clear days where the air seems to vibrate and the sun's rays feel mentholated.

783. I love eating popcorn at the movies, especially if I haven't eaten dinner.

784. I love napping in a parked car out in the driveway after a long drive home.

785. I love hearing wonderful stories about a person's life—too bad it's usually at their funeral.

786. I love seeing candid pictures of myself having a great time!

787. I love this Alfred Adler quote—"The only normal people are the one's you don't know very well."

788. I love finding new things to appreciate in old familiar routines.

789. I love rooms that have unusual shapes, nooks and crannies.

We have within us the capacity
to manufacture the very quality
we are constantly chasing.

— Daniel Gilbert

Love-Ability

When we say someone is "loveable" we usually mean they're charming, endearing, and provoke love in others. I began to see another way to interpret the word.

Love-ABLE—having the intention, the ability and the skill to love as much as possible. In other words, my *ability* to love is a measure of my Love-*Ability*.

The *LoveSpell Secret* was helping me increase my Love-*Ability*. And by growing my Love-*Ability* I became happier.

Around friends or strangers, I couldn't help but ask myself, "What do/can I love about this person?" Just asking the question provoked a silent answer that enhanced the connection between us. By looking for what made them loveable, I became more love-*able*.

AUGUST

790. I love chasing sunsets at 35,000 feet.

791. I love visiting Montana and kayaking on Whitefish Lake.

792. I love furniture made of rough-hewn wood that echoes Nature.

793. I love asking people what kind of tree they'd rather be—a maple that turns colors and loses its leaves every year or an evergreen?

794. I love power-boating across a lake—wind, foam, spray.

795. I love getting a massage, even if it hurts a little.

796. I love grinning all day while hiking spectacular Logan's Pass in Glacier National Park.

797. I love filling my water bottle from streams of glacial runoff and quenching my 6,600 ft thirst.

798. I love having a "close encounter" with a mountain goat and her baby.

799. I love sitting on a rock above Hidden Lake—my eyes feasting on its beauty, my mouth watering for a sandwich.

800. I love learning that only a forest fire can open the seeds in pinecones—fire and death create new life.

801. I love how dressing up as a cowboy with a six-gun and holster takes me back to being 7 years old.

802. I love how the wilderness of mountain glaciers calls me to visit the wild within me.

803. I love making a wish on a "blue moon"*—that rare occurrence of two full moons in the same month.

804. I love dancing the Hora at a Jewish wedding—especially under a tent on a ranch in Montana.

AUGUST

805. I love drinking champagne with a sprig of lavender that tickles my nose and taste buds.

806. I love being with twins—especially twin 5 year-old girls who finish each other's sentences.

807. I love eating chocolate pudding with pieces of bittersweet hiding inside.

808. I love doing the alpine slide on Big Mountain—twice!—screaming all the way down.

809. I love riding a chairlift up & down a mountain and feeling like an eagle.

810. I love the idea of a God that lives in Nature—in majestic places like Hidden Lake in Glacier National Park.

811. I love eating huckleberry ice cream, pie, everything, and understanding why NW Montana is huckleberry-crazy!

812. I love playing Pied Piper in a hotel's poolside hot tub—leading more and more kids in a game of Memory Mirror.

813. I love drinking wine lakeside—then buzzed, taking pictures of the spectacular sunset.

814. I love it when "problems" take care of themselves & seem to evaporate rather than having to be solved.

815. I love 1st person accounts of near-death experiences that puts quotes around the word "death."

816. I love returning things I've bought and feeling like I've found money.

817. I love listening to the chorus of bird chatter in the woods at dusk.

818. I love feeling my body getting stronger rather than weaker.

819. I love being told bedtime stories by a 4 year-old.

We are all born for love.

It is the principle of existence,

and its only end.

— Benjamin Disraeli

LoveSpell Circles

When I shared my *LoveSpell Experiment* with friends, some were inspired to try it themselves. To help them, I conceived a workbook—a 30-day program that would guide them to develop their own *LoveHabit* so they could create more love in their lives.

While working on the book, I began to envision groups of people getting together on a regular basis in *LoveSpell Circles*.

Having led a monthly Wisdom Circle for many years, I knew how powerful meeting regularly with a group of like-minded people could be. With each other's support and encouragement, participants would cast *LoveSpells* every day for 30 days and begin to experience the amazing benefits of the *LoveSpell Secret*.

SEPTEMBER

820. I love roaming wooded paths that Walt Whitman walked and basking in the same source of inspiration.

821. I love simple pleasures—a chorus of crickets in the evening, my Tweetheart's sighs at night and birdsong in the morning.

822. I love stories about triumphing over adversity—rising from the ashes like a Phoenix.

823. I love the convenience of online banking, especially when I'm traveling and have $$$ in my account.

824. I love people's endless creativity because it mirrors the Universe's infinite creation.

825. I love the varied career I've had—actor, artist, producer, author—so rich in creative expression.

826. I love profound SILENCE—the louder, the better!

827. I love when people look me in eye when passing by.

828. I love winning a book award• because it will hopefully lead to more sales and even more inspired souls.

829. I love getting hungry—it's like foreplay—especially when I know I can eat whenever I want.

830. I love sitting under a tree whose leaves are being rustled by the wind.

831. I love the Jewish New Year tradition of wishing everyone the happiest, healthiest and sweetest year yet!

832. I love the New Year opportunity to take soul stock and ask people I may have hurt for forgiveness.

833. I love sleeping on our new "luxury firm" mattress—it's hard so I can be soft.

834. I love not needing the "training wheels" of organized religion to feel a connection with the infinite.

• My memoir, *JOYride: How My Late Wife Loved Me Back To Life*, won an eLit Award—silver medal for Best Inspirational/Spiritual Digital Book of 2011.

835. I love the holiday foods that are eaten once a year much more than if I ate them frequently.

836. I love the way WIND brings Nature alive: through SOUND (leaves rustling), through MOVEMENT (branches swaying), and through TOUCH (the way it feels on my skin).

837. I love hunting for "buried treasure" with a 4 year-old: leaves, stones, twigs, even weeds are all so EUREKA!

838. I love dreaming about loved ones who are no longer here on the earth plane.

839. I love the quiet that ensues after a family-filled holiday weekend.

840. I love how MAKING LOVE can become a portal to the Infinite & the Divine.

841. I love it when green moss carpets the forest floor.

842. I love bidets and I'm not embarrassed to say it!

843. I love the challenge of finding new things to love—but I'm obviously stumped right now.

844. I love amusing myself—I'm probably my biggest fan!

845. I love how different styles of music create different moods.

846. I love thinking that the SOUL PURPOSE OF MONEY IS TO EXPRESS GRATITUDE!

847. I love being turned on to new things by people whose opinion & taste I value & trust.

848. I love the possibility that many of the world's religions are the result of contact with ETs.

849. I love cloudless days—especially here in the Northeast where they're rarer than they are back in LA.

850. I love getting silly with kids more than making small-talk with adults.

"Love your neighbor as yourself" — Leviticus 19:18
Even the Bible proclaims this the supreme commandment. But the Golden Rule begins with us... and what we love.

— I. J. Weinstock

The LoveSpell Challenge

As I put the finishing touches on the workbook, my vision of *LoveSpell Circles* evolved. After meeting weekly for a month sharing their *LoveSpells*, participants could choose to take *The LoveSpell Challenge*—declaring 1001 loves over the course of the year. Thus, embarking on their own *LoveSpell Experiment*.

Some may want to discover more of who they are through the unique "love-portrait" that will emerge. Others may be drawn, as the poet Rumi said, *"by the stronger pull of what you really love*" to discover their soul's purpose. Most may simply want to get themselves a pair of "love-colored glasses" through which to view their life.

And, of course, there will be those who—having increased their *Love-Ability*—will want to create more love in their life by finding a soulmate. A *LoveSpell Circle* is the perfect place to begin.

SEPTEMBER

851. I love what my TweetHeart said—"When we make love, I think of NOTHING and understand EVERYTHING!"

852. I love sitting on a stone jetty at the beach and watching seagulls dance around the big waves crashing into it.

853. I love hot saki, especially when the owner of a sushi bar treats me to some.

854. I love getting stuff delivered from Amazon to my doorstep, especially sooner than I expected.

855. I love pausing at the end of a breath and even resting in the space between breaths.

856. I love a cold drink on a hot day and a hot drink on a cold day—the Law of Relativity—so simple, so satisfying!

857. I love thinking that the word "hope" is an acronym—for example: Happy Options for the People of Earth.

858. I love when the house is filled with the aroma of cooking a delicious holiday meal.

859. I love wondering how documenting our lives with photos and videos—seeing ourselves age—is going to change our consciousness.

860. I love hearing kids laughing and screaming with glee as they play out on the lawn.

861. I love that children would rather be happy than hold a grudge in contrast to adults who'd rather be right than be happy.

862. I love the ritual of holidays that create a break from the day-to-day routines of life.

863. I love lighting a candle for a departed loved one to focus my mind, my heart and my memories.

864. I love this pearl from my TweetHeart—"I love kneading you!" she says as she gently double entendres me!

865. I love the challenge of finding the humor in suffering, especially my suffering—I can either laugh or cry.

866. I love my TweetHeart!—There I've said it!

SEPTEMBER

867. I love sitting in a maternity hospital waiting room with other expectant families receiving dispatches from the delivery room.

868. I love thinking of a hospital as a kind of soul port with happy "arrivals" and sad "departures."

869. I love witnessing a man's eyes fill with tears as he becomes a father and holds the tiny hand of his newborn son.

870. I love finally falling into bed after a sleepless night waiting for a baby to be born.

871. I love toasting & drinking & toasting & drinking & toasting & drinking to celebrate a new life.

872. I love the possibility that an eye doctor who dilates my pupils can see into the "windows of my soul."

873. I love kayaking at night on the Long Island Sound under a full moon.

874. I love the way GPS can reveal shortcuts and ways to avoid traffic that only the angels know.

875. I love telling my TweetHeart that I've traveled through Time to be with her—three time zones, that is!

876. I love the way most women are interested and most men try to be interesting.

877. I love checking things off my To Do List—it's very satisfying for a Capricorn to be productive.

878. I love my mattress because even though I may forget, my mattress holds all my memories.

879. I love when the moon smiles in the sky, sometimes even surprising me with a wink.

880. I love pasta—it's the epitome of culinary ingenuity and inspires so much creativity.

881. I love being on the floor—with a child, with a dog, with my soul in yoga & meditation.

In order for connection to happen,

we have to allow ourselves to be seen—really seen.

— Brené Brown

The LoveSpell Secret To Finding a Soulmate

Joy and I were a match-made-in-heaven. Literally.

In her memoir, *Love Ever After*, Joy described using the 12-Step program she'd been given by her late husband *after* he died to find new love. After six weeks, she found me.

To help other people find the love of their dreams, we created the *12 Steps to Finding Your Soulmate* workshop. I now saw how fundamental the *LoveSpell Secret* was to finding a soulmate.

One of the most important keys to finding your soulmate is *in-to-me-see,* better known as intimacy. To connect deeply with another, you have to first connect deeply with yourself. Discovering all the things you love is a powerful way to connect with yourself. Sharing your precious loves with another is a key to intimacy.

Most people believe that a soulmate is going to fix their life. The truth is you have to fix your own life before you're ready to meet your soulmate. Quite simply, the more you love your life, the more love-*able* you are. And the more you've loved your life into shape, the more you're ready to be someone's soulmate.

SEPTEMBER

882. I love the idea of basing your religion on which one has the most fun & entertaining holidays.

883. I love wrestling in the dark with my TweetHeart.

884. I love creating memorable milestones.

885. I love knowing that I take roughly 23 thousand breaths a day and 8.5 million breaths a year—the potential power of becoming conscious of my breath.

886. I love visiting a local street fair—eating hot corn-on-the-cob & going on fun carnival rides.

887. I love being surprised by the unexpected arrival of an old friend.

888. I love this Goldilocks planet of ours—not too hot, not too cold, just right!

889. I love the idea that the invisible ocean of cell transmissions is our new womb & I hope that it will birth a new & evolved human.

890. I love having a washing machine & dryer —I remember school days at the Laundromat.

891. I love getting "signs" after I've asked for guidance about which "road" to take.

892. I love this pearl from my TweetHeart— "Next to loving you, I love my GPS."

893. I love how persistence and perspiration leads to great performance.

894. I love an omelet, home fries, an English muffin and a cup of coffee for brunch.

895. I love the lessons—some hard, some easy— that living in two places—NY & LA—teaches me.

896. I love how resilient wilting plants can be when their thirst is quenched—we can learn from them.

897. I love how at brunch the men argued about the Existence of God while the women gossiped about Infidelities and a recent Marital Scandal.

SEPTEMBER

898. I love wondering which biblical tale we're reenacting—eating the forbidden Apple in the Garden of Eden or building the Tower of Babel?

899. I love listening to radio—it's so intimate.

900. I love seeing the amazement & wonder in a toddler's eyes.

901. I love those things that are like oxygen to the soul—hope, gratitude and love.

902. I love how easy it is today to get one's message out into the world.

903. I love watching two birds flying together across the sky—there's something inspiring about any couple.

904. I love the Zen master's saying—"Let go...or get dragged!"

905. I love remembering that Adversity is like a University where great lessons are learned.

906. I love those moments in life when we see the big picture—how NOW connects to something that happened 20 years ago.

907. I love how getting older makes your mortality an energizing presence—it often hangs in the air like morning dew.

908. I love imagining different ways I could love my world more.

909. I love the new possibilities created by a neat and clean desk—I'll try to experience it more often.

910. I love being reminded of things I used to love—it's one of the perks of organizing one's closets.

911. I love Schopenhauer's 3 stages of Truth—1st it's ridiculed, 2nd it's violently opposed & 3rd it's accepted as being self-evident.

912. I love drawings that use tiny hand drawn words as brushstrokes illustrating what the words describe.

Life is a challenge, meet it!

Life is a dream, realize it!

Life is a game, play it!

Life is love, enjoy it!

— Sai Baba

A Treasure Hunt

From the time I was a child, I've felt that life consisted of the "games" we choose to play. Perhaps that's why in the early '90's I created a new cable network called The Game Channel which was the precursor to GSN (The Game Show Network).

Casting a *LoveSpell* was also a game, a kind of treasure hunt. Now I was hunting for the buried treasure of the 1001 things I loved.

We all have a 1001 things we love. One of the most fulfilling games of life, I was discovering, is to find and declare them.

There were days I saw myself playing other games. One day I was a Love Detective gathering the evidence. On another day I felt like a Love Hunter stalking my prey.

OCTOBER

913. I love wondering if the NEXT BIG THING will STAND THE TEST OF TIME?

914. I love the irony that we increasingly compensate for the lack of Nature in our lives with a pill or app.

915. I love storage units—they're a mixed blessing for flawed human beings like myself.

916. I love REMEMBERING and I love FORGETTING—I'm grateful for both.

917. I love GENEROSITY—giving & receiving—it's one of the engines of Love.

918. I love how a magnifying glass makes the small appear large and a telescope makes the far seem near.

919. I love having experts to advise me—a doctor about my health and an accountant about my wealth.

920. I love that there's a key for every lock and if you lose that key there's always a lock cutter.

921. I love this quote from William Blake—"It is easier to forgive an enemy than to forgive a friend."

922. I love the different meanings of rhyming words—prophets value God, profits value $.

923. I love the idea of everyone in the world taking a picture at the same time.

924. I love pickles (half sour) & sauerkraut to give a meal a certain deli-ciousness.

925. I love a new spelling for WONDERFUL—it's ONEDERFUL to feel connected to everything!

926. I love the fortune cookie I got last night—"Every wise man started out asking many questions."

927. I love the wit & wisdom in this saying—"Love is blind, but marriage is a real eye-opener."

928. I love glimpsing the shadow of a leaf falling to the ground—so simple, symbolic & sublime.

OCTOBER

929. I love walks down memory lane and visions of the future.

930. I love learning that in China there's a Street of Eternal Happiness and in America there's a town called Boring.

931. I love being inspired when I'm going through a tough passage by the knowledge that all birth is a painful process.

932. I love hearing that 1 in 5 children claim to see "ghosts" or what they often call their "imaginary friends."

933. I love finding somewhere to take a stand—planted there I can move the world!

934. I love working my way thru a pile of To Do's.

935. I love creating an altar that reminds me of the varied facets of my soul.

936. I love pineapple more than most other fruits except bananas.

937. I love questions that make me think, for ex: If I could say one thing to every human being in the world, what would I say?

938. I love my DVR—watching when I want, fast-forwarding, rewinding and commercial-free.

939. I love having balance, especially when someone I love loses theirs.

940. I love having a large painted butterfly weather vane on the roof to tell me which way the wind is blowing.

941. I love "golden time"—sunset, dusk, twilight—it's the magic of being between the worlds of day & night.

942. I love counting my breaths—it demands my presence in the NOW.

943. I love learning that it's possible "civilization" goes back much further in time than we've been led to believe.

944. I love myths and fairy tales—they speak to a deeper truth than so-called "reality."

Love absolutely everything

that ever happens in your life.

— Paul Cantalupo

The LoveSpell Game

One of the great things about casting a *LoveSpell* is that it's so simple a child can do it. In fact, children *should* do it—it's as important for them as learning to brush their teeth.

The more I thought about it, the more convinced I became that the *LoveSpell Secret* should be turned into a game—the *LoveSpell Game*—so that children can play it.

To that end I wrote some children's stories that I hoped would intrigue kids with the magical possibilities of the *LoveSpell Secret* . I planned a series of children's books for both boys and girls that would make playing the *LoveSpell Game* fun and exciting.

Playing the *LoveSpell Game* with a child—at the kitchen table, while putting them to bed, or in the car—is a fun way to train them to look at life through "love-colored glasses." If children master the *LoveSpell Game*, they'll reap the amazing benefits that a daily dose of Vitamin L provides for the rest of their lives.

OCTOBER

945. I love some things slow and some things fast, some things cold and some things hot.

946. I love imagining what the $2 billion the presidential candidates are spending could buy for those less fortunate.

947. I love the innocent & idealistic 12 year-old boy still living inside of me.

948. I love the bumper sticker "Love Wins!"

949. I love knowing that fear is nothing to be afraid of but rather a way to know what you're made of.

950. I love watching leaves fall to the ground—it feels almost sacred like someone dying.

951. I love the sound of the word "capricious" but not what it means—fickle fate.

952. I love knowing that HYPOCRISY is the homage that VICE pays to VIRTUE.

953. I love holding out the possibility that "destruction" can be experienced as a "cleansing and purification."

954. I love believing I can't fail and that the wind will always fill my sails.

955. I love the lyric—"I tried, but don't remember how I died."

956. I love seeing my body as a "temple" fed by sacred rivers—blood, lymph—where my soul makes pilgrimages beneath the sun of my mind and the moon of my emotions.

957. I love turning a corner, turning a page, turning over a new leaf—especially in the Fall.

958. I love imagining humans had tails like dogs so we'd know when we were happy—Oh what tails we would tell!

959. I love focusing on living the depth of my life and not simply the length of it.

960. I love how the warrior rejects the concept of SURRENDER while the lover yearns for it.

961. I love that after wading thru piles of paper on my desk I can actually see the wood.

OCTOBER

962. I love watching the crazy antics new parents will go to get their kids to smile for the camera.

963. I love what the 108 yr old Holocaust survivor said was the secret to her longevity—"I look for the good."

964. I love LA & wonder if the pilgrims had landed in California, whether the East Coast would still be a wilderness?

965. I love unexpectedly stumbling upon a poetry reading where my mind is gently massaged by carefully chosen words.

966. I love this advice about religious debate—It's useless to attempt to reason someone out of a thing he was never reasoned into.

967. I love those times I utter a word I've never said before.

968. I love that "hear" + t = "heart." So to come from the heart, you have to use your ear to hear & listen.

969. I love that the symphony of our lives is played by neurons, muscles, cells & heartstrings.

970. I love standing at a crossroads and saying an emphatic "Yes" to one of the paths.

971. I love the expression "getting my Zen on!"

972. I love finally facing a fear—even though I resisted until resistance was futile.♥

973. I love distinguishing between comfort & happiness—not mistaking one for the other.

974. I love cleaning out YEARS of "stuff" that's piled up in storage.

975. I love NOT sinking, even though the last few days I've sprung a leak & been taking on water.

976. I love that the antidote for Oy is Joy!

♥ I finally had enough of bi-coastaling. Though I loved LA and dreaded the logistical nightmare of moving cross-country, I decided it was time to sell my home and relocate to LI so Lilly and I could build a life together.

Pollyana & the Glad Game

It was only a matter of time before someone told me that the *LoveSpell Secret* reminded them of The Glad Game they'd played as a child, and that it had been one of their favorite games.

Unfamiliar with The Glad Game, I did a little research and learned that it was introduced in a 1913 best-selling novel, *Pollyana*, by Eleanor H. Porter. I'd heard the term Pollyana but wasn't familiar with the story.

Pollyana, an 11 year-old orphan, goes to live with her wealthy but stern Aunt. To play the Glad Game (which she learned from her father), Polyanna has to find something to be glad about in every situation. Playing the Glad Game protects Pollyana from her strict Aunt. For example, when her Aunt puts her in an attic room without carpets or pictures, Pollyana focuses on the beautiful view from the window.

One by one, Pollyanna teaches some of the town's unhappiest people to play the game. Even her Aunt can't resist Pollyanna's optimism. Ultimately, Pollyana transforms her aunt's depressing New England town into a pleasant place to live.

Pollyana became a classic of children's literature and was such a success that there were more than a dozen sequels and several film versions.

The term *Pollyana* has become synonymous for someone with an overly optimistic disposition. Used disparagingly, it can refer to someone whose optimism is naïve and almost delusional.

I was delighted to discover that by casting a *LoveSpell* I'd been playing an adult version of The Glad Game. And it confirmed my feeling that its simplicity made it ideal for children. But I also had to wonder—was I, in the disparaging sense of the word, a Pollyana? My life had been a journey from Oy to Joy, but....

I read about the famous writer Ray Bradbury, author of *Fahrenheit 451*, who described himself as being half Pollyanna and half Cassandra, seeing only the good in the present while making dire warnings about the future. Not bad company, I thought.

Love life and life will love you back.

— Arthur Rubinstein

OCTOBER

977. I love being man enough to sit with the women.

978. I love the idea that GRIEVANCES & INJUSTICES should be written in sand, while ACTS OF LOVE are written in stone!

979. I love taking pictures and plan on putting the best together in a book so that I can see all that I've seen.

980. I love fresh, clean towels though I prefer sheets that have already been slept in.

981. I love how the Thesaurus helps me find creative ways of saying the same thing.

982. I love being a glutton for pleasure.

983. I love thinking of consciousness as a filter through which we see the world—there are dog filters, dove filters and lots of human filters.

984. I love that we have the same number of genes as chickens and fruit flies—there's even genetic similarity between jellyfish and humans.

985. I love eating ripe figs with certain cheeses. Mmmm!

986. I love when my TweetHeart says I surprise her, especially when I'm just being myself.

987. I love imagining the 90% of "reality" that's invisible to the naked eye.

988. I love encouraging people to "sing their song" so they don't leave this world with their song still inside them.

989. I love it when the people around me are happy—but it's their responsibility, not mine.

990. I love creating wholeness—like embracing one's shadow—because ultimately it's holy.

991. I love exercising my discipline—like saying No to Twizzlers, M&Ms and a 2nd helping of ice cream.

992. I love how my morning shower can be a portal into infinite reasons for gratitude.

OCTOBER

993. I love that the minute I realized my dog was gone, I received a call from someone who'd found him.

994. I love that the pineal gland in the middle of our brain has retinal cells—scientific proof of our spiritual 3rd Eye.

995. I love Einstein's quote about Knowledge versus Imagination—knowledge is limited by what we know but imagination is unlimited.

996. I love being accused of "excessive positivity."

997. I love meeting a woman who admits to having a sexual fantasy about Larry David.

998. I love having my mind blown by something beautiful, surprising, touching, amazing, once-in-a-lifetime-ing.

999. I love saying NO to what doesn't feel right; it allows more room for the YES's in my life.

1000. I love that every cell in our body is like a light bulb and has a spiraling wire—a conduit for light—that we call our DNA.

OCTOBER

1001. I love the idea of describing someone who's died as taking "an eternity leave."

1002. I love depositing 1001 loves in my LoveBank—I feel so enriched!

1003. I love fortune cookies after a Chinese meal—what a wonderful tradition.

1004. On someone's birthday I love congratulating their mother on her Birth Day.

1005. I love being here & now, especially when there's a natural disaster there.

1006. I love the Weather Channel when I'm far away from loved ones who are suffering through bad weather.

1007. I love finally hearing from loved ones who are in the midst of a natural disaster.♥

♥ I'd returned to LA to prep my home before putting it on the market. The day before my scheduled return to LI, Lilly suffered through Hurricane Sandy. She was without power and a tree had fallen on (not through) her roof. My scheduled return flight was cancelled due to NY airports being closed. In addition, my brother lived in Tribeca, a part of lower Manhattan that was flooded and without power, too.

If only you could love enough,

you would be the happiest

and most powerful being in the universe.

— Emmett Fox

A LoveBank

I became increasingly aware that there was yet another benefit to casting a *LoveSpell*—beyond the self-portrait that emerged, the numbers grew.

With each love declaration, I felt enriched—as if I was putting money in the bank. A *LoveBank!* How would it feel to deposit a thousand and one loves? Ten Thousand? What would it feel like to be a *Love-illionaire?*

If I'd been taught the *LoveSpell Secret* as a child—like Pollyana was taught the Glad Game—I'd have built up quite a *LoveBank* account. What impact would it have on my life? How enriched would I feel today?

According to researcher Barbara Frederickson, people can actually "bank" their positive emotions to help them through tough times. The reason why is that "the small investments you deposit in the so-called bank don't just sit there. They accumulate, earn interest, and pay out dividends in the form of durable resources that you can later draw on to face future adversity."

So the more *LoveSpells* I banked, the more resilient I would be. Like a rainy-day fund, my *LoveBank* could be drawn on to help me deal with any misfortune.

NOVEMBER

1008. I love the "hero" in me who acts in spite of fear.

1009. I love whatever it is that inspires first responders to go TOWARDS a crisis and not AWAY from it.

1010. I love that LOVE inspires me to fly from LA to power-less LI to be with my TweetHeart.

1011. I love the challenge of discovering the "gifts & blessings" that can ultimately emerge from a "tragedy." •

1012. I love how people come together when faced with a disaster.

1013. I love sleeping with my TweetHeart after not seeing her for three weeks.

1014. I love candlelight, especially when the power is out and it's dark at night.

• I hope those who were devastated by Hurricane Sandy are not offended by my attempt to find things to love about my experience of the disaster. Here was a real world test of my *LoveSpell Experiment.* In retrospect, I realize that we had a relatively easy time of it compared to many others.

NOVEMBER

1015. In a disaster I love all the food in the pantry I never bothered with like oatmeal and sardines.

1016. I love being reminded of things I've taken for granted—like electricity and all that it powers.

1017. In the powerless wake of Hurricane Sandy, I love continuing to cast a LoveSpell every day even if I can't get online to tweet it.

1018. In the wake of the storm, I love peanut butter and any food that doesn't have to be refrigerated.

1019. In the wake of the storm, I love so many new things because I've lost them temporarily.

1020. I love Laundromats with power & wi-fi when our power is still out and we've run out of clean towels.

1021. I love chainsaws, especially when a tree is down and threatening to fall through the roof.

NOVEMBER

1022. I love the way people bond in the wake of a natural disaster—we're all in the same leaking boat.

1023. I love boiled water and how necessary it is to food and eating in a winter without power.

1024. Without power and heat, I love sitting in front of the wood-burning stove now more than ever.

1025. I love the paradoxical ways that losing electrical power can be personally empowering!

1026. I love finding a public place like the local art movie theater where those without power could gather to watch the election returns.

1027. I love how my reaction to the loss of power (more than 10 days now) evokes waves of gratitude that it wasn't worse.

1028. I love having the power back on—the light & heat & all the comforts of an electrified home.

1029. I love the overwhelming feelings of GRATITUDE I feel after being WITHOUT power for 11 days.

1030. I love noticing and being grateful for all the things I usually took for granted before the storm.

1031. I love water—I can't say it enough—to drink, wash, cook, clean. It's "liquid love!"

1032. I love pickles—half-sour with garlic—with a sandwich or even by itself.

1033. I love being reminded of the simple things—one of the silver linings of losing power from a storm.

1034. I love knowing that bad decisions, mistakes, even tragedies can make great stories.

1035. I love this advice—Try something three times: once to get over the fear; twice to learn how; three times to figure out whether you like it.

1036. I love learning that it's my attitude that gives me shelter from the storm.

Here is my secret. It is very simple:

It is only with the heart

that one can see rightly;

what is essential is invisible to the eye."

— Antoine de Saint-Exupéry
"The Little Prince"

A Child Shall Lead Them

The Old Testament prophet Isaiah prophesied a coming Golden Age—a future time of universal peace and brotherhood without crime, war and poverty.

> *"The wolf also shall dwell with the lamb, and the leopard shall lie down with the kid; and the calf and the young lion and the fatling together; and* a little child shall lead them." (Isaiah 11:6)

I was reminded of the child-like simplicity yet profound impact of the *LoveSpell Secret.* Because it's so deceptively simple, the *LoveSpell Secret* seems like something only a child would do—a Glad Game. But that's the secret!

In myth and fairy tale, the treasure, the healing elixir, the great blessing is always hidden in plain sight, often under the nose of busy adults yet where children and the child-like can see.

After searching the world—seeking high and low, far and wide—the hero often finds the treasure at home where it's always been. After returning from Oz, didn't Dorothy say, "There's no place like home, there's no place like home!"

The child-like simplicity of casting a *LoveSpell* hides its secret power to magically transform one's life.

NOVEMBER

1037. I love drinking hot sake on a cold November night to celebrate having power again in our home.

1038. I love imagining the renewal of Spring as I walk through devastated woods with so many trees downed by the storm.

1039. I love feeling better after being sick with a stomach bug for the last 48 hrs.

1040. I love finding a silver lining in disappointment—it's a necessary life-skill they should teach in school.

1041. I love interpreting a solar eclipse as a harbinger of great change.

1042. I love being healthy again so that I can appreciate the infinite other loves that are available to me.

1043. I love my dreams—especially the ones where I know I'm dreaming.

1044. I love feeling hungry again and being able to keep food down—three cheers for my immune system!

1045. I love finding unlikely things to be grateful for—a speeding ticket as a "wake-up call" or a cold as an opportunity for R&R.

1046. I love how creative I become when I have to soothe an unhappy toddler.

1047. I love participating more than spectating—for me that's where the juice is!

1048. I love the sound of fallen leaves crunching beneath my feet.

1049. I love mashed potatoes—there's something so comforting about them!

1050. I love the idea that there are PASSWORDS TO LIFE—words like HOPE, GENEROSITY, FREEDOM and, of course, LOVE.

1051. I love visiting a children's museum and exploring all the hands-on exhibits where you can play.

1052. I love how football has become America's secular "religion."

NOVEMBER

1053. I love eating hot oatmeal with all the fixings on a cold, rainy morning.

1054. I love wearing jackets, sweaters, coats in cold NY that I never wore in warm LA.

1055. I love magnifying articles on my computer so it's easier to read.

1056. I love the saying "Everything has beauty, but not everyone sees it" and paraphrase "Everything is loveable, but not everyone can love it."

1057. I love sharing a bottle of good wine with friends over a birthday dinner celebration.

1058. I love the image of woman flowing like a river while man provides the riverbanks.

1059. I love seeing how much better things could be, yet being aware of how much there is to be grateful for.

1060. I love shopping for children's toys—both for the children in my life and the deprived "inner child" in me.

1061. I love talking Infantese & Toddlerish which are all dialects of the Language of Love.

1062. I love when a group of adults spontaneously begin to sing a song from their childhood.

1063. I love participating in a beautiful global candle-lighting for children who've died.

1064. I love fog-enshrouded streets—they're mysterious and make me feel like I'm in a movie.

1065. I love instant replays—slow-mo from every angle—that let you see what really happened.

1066. I love chocolate brownies—who doesn't?!

1067. I love wondering what it feels like to be a tree in Autumn as my leaves die & fall to the ground?

1068. I love an impromptu game of pool with family...and winning!

1069. I love getting quiet enough to hear that unique thing that makes me tick.

We are made by love, we are made of love,
and we are made for love!
Everything is love anyway.
Our hate is love turned sour,
jealousy is love turned bitter,
our fears are love standing upside down,
greed is love gone overboard,
attachment is love gone sticky.

— Khurshed Batliwala

I Love, Therefore I Am!

It's been said that when we face death, our wealth, our success, even the knowledge we've gained over a lifetime matters little. What remains in those last precious moments of life is the singular realization of the importance of love.

A friend, after being pronounced dead for nearly a half-hour, returned from her near-death experience proclaiming *Love is all there is!*

The ancient Egyptians believed that after we die, our souls undergo a life-review in which we're asked two questions: *Did you love? Were you loved?*

Ultimately, it is love that defines us—*I love, therefore I am!*

NOVEMBER

1070. I love standing beneath a skylight in a pool of full moonlight hugging my TweetHeart.

1071. I love those moments when I feel as though I'm a "servant of love."

1072. I love watching water or soup boil, since A WATCHED POT NEVER BOILS.

1073. I love the irony that more may be gained by stillness than by action.

1074. I love taking a bath with my TweetHeart and dancing in the water to a world beat.

1075. I love hearing about great acts of forgiveness—they're like moral mountains to climb.

1076. Sometimes I love sharing soul more than saliva, sharing kindness more than a kiss.

1077. I love my morning shower!—I can't say it enough—it's a luxury even the Kings, Emperors & Pharaohs of old would envy.

1078. I love my TweetHeart telling me that I make her feel like the first woman—Eve.

1079. I love living my life so that my regrets will be about things I've done rather than things I didn't do.

1080. I love Nietzsche's quote: "And those who were seen dancing were thought to be insane by those who could not hear the music."

1081. I love it when parents talk to their kids about the two dreaded topics—sex & death.

1082. I love wildlife videos of the unlikely friendship between PREDATOR & PREY —leopard & monkey, fox & rabbit—who bonded at birth.

1083. I love to eat food in which you can taste the cook's love.

1084. I love that I can't step into the same river twice—I'm not the same nor is the river—there is nothing permanent except change.

1085. I love when my TweetHeart makes love and begins speaking to me in clitorish.

NOVEMBER

1086. I love the irony that Thanksgiving occurs when there's little daylight, warmth or crops—when we're most in need of gratitude.

1087. I love holidays because they're holy-days—taking us out of the day-to-day so we can cherish what's really important.

1088. I love Thanksgiving more than any other holiday because it's all about GRATITUDE, not presents.

1089. I love the side dishes of Thanksgiving—cranberry sauce, sweet potatoes and pumpkin cheesecake—more than the turkey.

1090. I love that Thanksgiving, unlike most holidays, has nothing to do with God.

1091. I love that Thanksgiving, unlike other holidays, has its roots in Native American culture.

1092. I love banana bread, I also love bananas and I love bread, too. I'm incoherent from all the holiday food.

1093. I love the old woman's advice on who to marry—"A lot happens in life. Smart, fun and a big heart will get you through all of it."

1094. I love using the term "Source" instead of "God"—God has so much baggage while Source is so inclusive suggesting Oneness.

1095. I love a good dinner party—eight people, great food, interesting conversation—it doesn't get any better!

1096. I love meditations in which I experience my self as an eddy in a stream.

1097. I love contemplating the inconceivable—a day in the future when the monetization of life includes metering the air we breathe.

1098. I love this mother's gentle reprimand to her child—"Don't yuk someone's yum!" We can all take it to heart.

1099. I love those moments when I murmur "Thank You" with each exhalation of my breath.

As I grow to understand life less and less,

I learn to love it more and more.

— Jules Renard

You Are What You Love

We've all heard the expression, "You are what you eat!" In a similar vein, "You are what you love!"

Love nourishes us the way sunlight nourishes plants, and the way oxygen, food and water nourish animals. Without the essential nutrient of love, we wither away.

That's why it's so important to focus on Love—to look for and find love in everything and everyone. We spend too much time and energy judging, blaming, and condemning—in other words focusing on what's *wrong*. We need to reprogram ourselves to look for the love in as much of our life as we can because it is our most essential nutrient.

DECEMBER

1100. I love how the urge to light candles grows—and is celebrated—as we move into the darkest part of the year.

1101. I love getting my beard trimmed after way too long.

1102. I love the realization that there's only "good" & "for the good" (more commonly known as "bad").

1103. I love wondering what drum is so large that it's only beaten once every hundred years? And by whom?

1104. I love the paradox that if you see your path laid out in front of you, it's not your path since you make your path with every step you take.

1105. I love how iPads & smartphones are for some a nightlight, a candle in the wind, even a lighthouse beacon in the storm.

1106. I love ice cream cake, any kind of coconut pastry, then top it off with fruit.

1107. I love that in an age where the word "friend" is a verb, we still have Close Encounters of the Kindred Kind.

1108. I love that if I'm waiting for the cavalry or some hero to save the day, all I have to do is look into the mirror.

1109. I love laughing so hard I think I'm going to swallow a lung.

1110. I love having survived several "Dark Nights of the Soul."

1111. I love that I've finally come to accept and even embrace most of my faults, flaws and weaknesses.

1112. I love that people don't know how strong they are until they find themselves—like teabags—in hot water.

1113. I love the paradox that to feel connected, I sometimes have to be isolated.

1114. I love the natural reflections in a rain-soaked street, a puddle, a still lake.

DECEMBER

1115. Now that I'm wintering in LI instead of LA, I love gloves & scarves—things I haven't worn in decades.

1116. I love how the cold drives one inside in every respect—winter is the time to hibernate and dive deeper into the cave of oneself.

1117. I love when death takes a holiday and someone miraculously escapes with their life.

1118. I love watching the dog sprawl in front of the fire.

1119. I love being able to view the difficult people in my life as my greatest teachers.

1120. I love how my dog teaches me non-judgment—for him the good life means STOP & SMELL THE SHIT!

1121. I love that as a child I wanted things to last forever, but as I've grown older, I accept impermanence and am often grateful for change.

1122. I love that the East developed technologies for exploring Spirit long before the West developed technologies for exploring Matter.

1123. Every time my TweetHeart asks me to help her with her PC computer, I'm reminded how much I love my MAC.

1124. I love when a restaurant treats me with a surprise appetizer and even another glass of wine "on the house."

1125. I love escalators—not just the ride but the visual experience and even the sculptural effect.

1126. I love that NOW is the edge of ETERNITY —like the Illusion of Time Zones in different longitudes—it's all the same Earth time: NOW.

1127. I love knowing that the time I enjoy wasting isn't really wasted time.

1128. I love how my TweetHeart blesses me when I sneeze—instead of the usual "Bless you!" she says "I love you!"

Eventually you will come to understand

that love heals everything,

and love is all there is.

— Gary Zukav

The One True Religion

It dawned on me that Joy's question "What do you love?" was leading me on a sacred quest to enter and ultimately occupy my heart.

For many of the world's great religions, it's the heart not the mind that's revered. The Hindu Vedas refer to the "lotus in the heart," the Sufis—the mystical sect of Islam—speak of a "diamond in the heart," and for Christianity it's the "sacred heart."

In my humble opinion, *Love* is the one true religion. When I love, I align with the *Source of All That Is*. Many people call that *God*.

For the atheists out there, forget God, Love doesn't need a god! The *LoveSpell Secret* works whatever your beliefs. It's simple—your loves are like candles in the darkness waiting to be lit by your attention, appreciation, and acknowledgement. The more you love in your life, the more love you will see, and the happier you will be!

DECEMBER

1129. I love that living the spiritual life requires less & less, while the material life requires more & more.

1130. I love states of grace—what if someday we became the United States of Grace?

1131. Having written books about the power of questions, I love Voltaire's quote—"Judge a man by his questions rather than by his answers."

1132. I love my TweetHeart's comic complaint—"I need to take supplements for my memory but can't remember which they are."

1133. I love balancing between these 2 truths—the only constant is change & the more things change, the more they stay the same.

1134. I love surviving society's conflicting conditioning about sex—it's an awful, filthy thing & you should save it for someone you love.

1135. I love acting as if "someday" is today and every day!

1136. I love the analogy that 400 Americans having more wealth than 150 million is like cancer—wild growth at the expense of the social body's health & harmony.

1137. I love that I've never stopped asking the ORIGINAL QUESTION: Who & What am I?

1138. I love the myth of Narcissus warning us about the dangers of being enchanted by the reflections of our digital civilization.

1139. I love the imaginative possibilities that such a rare and auspicious date as 12/12/12 creates.

1140. I love the fearless adventurer in me who's often taken the ROAD LESS TRAVELLED, gotten lost for awhile, yet found my way home.

1141. I love those rare moments when I stop seeking & find God hiding inside of me.

1142. I love how visiting a cemetery where your loved ones are buried brings the dead to life.

DECEMBER

1143. I love the comfort, nurture, haven & contemplation, massage & meditation of my morning shower.

1144. I love how the bare tree branches in winter are bronchial-shaped—of course, they are the planet's lungs

1145. I love hot water whenever I turn on the tap—especially in winter—what a luxury!

1146. I love having journeyed over the course of my life from being NOT ENOUGH to MORE THAN ENOUGH.

1147. I love basking in the warm sunlight streaming through the window on a cold winter's day.

1148. I love that each of these daily LoveSpells are "inchstones" rather than milestones—easier to do and ultimately more impactful.

1149. I love the dusting of snow in LI—pretty without the hazard—that I never saw in LA.

1150. I love coming in out of the cold, feeling my face flush in the cozy warmth of the house.

1151. I love being willing to get pricked by thorns in order to smell the rose—Ahhh!

1152. I love the distinction that intelligence results from education while wisdom results from experience.

1153. I love finally figuring a new place out—but by then you usually have to leave. Life's a lot like that, too.

1154. I love my delusions & wear them like armor to protect me from the so-called "realists" of the world.

1155. I love how meditation makes me aware of my "monkey mind" with all its "buts," and also of my butt.

1156. I love standing out in the snow & catching snowflakes in my mouth—feeling them melting on my tongue—just like the dog.

The happy man is he who lives the life of love,
not for the honors it may bring, but for the life itself.

— R.J. Baughan

A Form of Prayer

Some may view my *LoveSpell Experiment* as the epitome of self-involvement—a monumental exercise in navel-gazing. To which I reply that, like Gandhi, I believe all change in the world begins with me. It's an inside job.

I began to see casting a *LoveSpell* as something sacred. By simply asking the question—*What Do I Love?*—I was creating a "sacred pause" from my habitual state of mind. *What do I love?* was as good a mantra as any.

Beating the drum for love every day throughout the day felt like a chant, an incantation, even a prayer.

What greater praise can we give the Creator than to discover all the things we love? What more fitting act of worship than to love more and more of our life?

DECEMBER

1157. I love DH Lawrence's advice—"Find a woman you can fall in love with. If you have not done so, you are wasting your life."

1158. I love that—though there have been times in my life that I lay whimpering in fear like a wounded dog—I've never been happier.

1159. I love how meditation draws me from compulsive DOING & HAVING to appreciating just BEING.

1160. I love Seinfeld's take on how amazing a joke is—like some treasure you save in a box in case of war.

1161. I love the magic created by persistence—NEVER GIVE UP!

1162. I love how empowering it can be to follow every hopeless "I can't ____" with a hopeful "but I can____."

1163. I love being safe & sheltered inside when the wind howls outside.

1164. I love waking up to a 6" snowfall that transforms the world into a winter wonderland.

1165. I love inspiring someone, especially a child, to ask "how?" or "why?"

1166. I love the William Blake quote—"If the doors of perception were cleansed, every thing would appear to man as it is, infinite."

1167. I love watching my golden retriever roll around in the snow—talk about having fun!

1168. I love that the difference between being in the SHIFT or the SHIT is an F—FREEDOM.

1169. I love having chosen TIME over MONEY as my guiding principle since it's the best investment of my limited TIME ON EARTH.

1170. I love not worrying about the "mistakes" in my wake and seeing them as "lessons."

1171. I love Swedenborg's quote—"Love in its essence is spiritual fire." Burn baby burn!

DECEMBER

1172. I love knowing I can never be bored—life is endlessly fascinating & the imaginative possibilities infinite.

1173. I love lighting a candle today in memory of my mother and feeling infinite gratitude for how much she loved me.

1174. I love how my TweetHeart said "I have to get up!" this morning then got out of bed, walked to the other side & got back in.

1175. I love how week-old snow looks like a whipped-cream topping on the landscape.

1176. I love those moments when I've known "equanimity"—accepting the "good" and the "bad" equally.

1177. I love when strangers open up to me like the taxicab driver who's "obsessed" with the color pink.

1178. I love the irony that surveillance cameras are everywhere recording people who are fixated on their hand-held screens.

1179. I love living, according to the Mayan Calendar, at the end of the Great Cosmic Year. •

1180. I love getting all these invitations to 12/21/12 "End of the World" parties—makes me hope the party never ends!

1181. I love the symbolic appeal of the End of the World. Chance to start over!

1182. On this Mayan-prophesied End-Birth of the World Day, I love what the Mayans said in greeting—"I am another you."

1183. I love imagining that the end of the Mayan Calendar today is NOT the end of the planet, but the end of business-as-usual.

1184. I love how the world-as-we-know-it ENDS every day as our Digital Global Mind creates new IDEAS & FILTERS with which to perceive new worlds.

• Supposedly our sun and solar system take approximately 26,000 years to make one revolution of our spiraling galaxy, the Milky Way. This is called The Great Year.

Love is the substance of all life.
Everything is connected in love,
absolutely everything.

— Julia Cameron

The Source is Love, Love is the Source

When I drill down deep enough, I find that love is the source of *everything*.

Most of our food is the product or "fruit" of an incredibly complex dance of the pollination of flowers by bees. This pollination is the sexual way flowering plants reproduce. If that isn't love in action, I don't know what is.

Water, the source of life, created by the immense attraction of hydrogen and oxygen atoms for each other can be seen as a product of love. Whenever we eat and drink, we are, in effect, being nurtured by love.

Tribal cultures around the world refer to plants, animals, and humans as the children of Father Sky and Mother Earth. They view Nature as an infinitely complex Dance of Love.

Even Gravity—which keeps our feet on the ground, holds the solar system in place and our Milky Way galaxy together—is a form of love on a grand cosmic scale.

Everything humans have created was dreamed, then loved into existence—from art to asphalt. The act of creation is an act of love!

Perhaps our ultimate goal during our brief time on this blue jewel of a planet is to love everything in our lives. Maybe that's the reason why we're here.

DECEMBER

1185. I love surviving the End of the World and being part of the New World, Fifth Sun, Aquarian Age. Whatever!

1186. I love the synchronicity that my new book, *The LoveSpell Secret*, was published today—Day 1 of the New Age.♥

1187. I love that the days are growing longer, more and more light, minute by minute, until the Summer Solstice.

1188. I love that I've immatured with age and that coming from the right place now means not the hip, but the heart.

1189. I love contemplating the WHY of LIFE—it leads me to doubting the WHAT of DEATH.

1190. I love knowing that how people treat you is THEIR karma but how you react is YOURS.

1191. I love hearing people, especially babies, squeal with delight.

♥ I published the workbook, *The LoveSpell Secret: A 30-Day Heaven-Sent Program to Create More Love in Your Life*, to help people create the habit of asking and answering one of the most important questions in life—*What Do You Love?*

1192. I love knowing that my thoughts and beliefs can be as imprisoning as an actual jail cell.

1193. I love being able to walk to restaurants, shops, drugstores and fruit markets as part of my daily life.

1194. I love thinking of smart phones as soothing pacifiers for adults or simply virtual "imaginary friends."

1195. One of the things I love about Christmas is experiencing that giving is so fulfilling.

1196. I love that the holidays are a way to celebrate the greatest miracle of life—Love!

1197. During Xmas, I love celebrating the wonder of everything or rather the One-der of Everything.

1198. This holiday season I love that I'm happy because Christmas is a bad time to have a hard time, a tough time to shed a tear.

DECEMBER

1199. I love having a 3-minute $1 chair-massage at the mall—can't beat the value.

1200. Speaking about malls, I love returning a gift and finding just the thing I need in exchange.

1201. I love the end of the year reminder that everything ends, so just relax and LET GO.

1202. I love the countdown to the New Year—harnessing the energies of new beginnings.

1203. I love all these year-end collections—best of's in music, art, film, books, etc.

1204. I love kissing my TweetHeart—it's as good as dessert and there's no calories. I'm going on the Kissing Diet!

1205. I love knowing the top searches of 2012, but disappointed it was Kim Kardashian & Justin Bieber.

1206. I love what my TweetHeart said—"One of the good things about getting older is that I won't remember my New Year's Resolution."

1207. I love looking back at New Year's Eves past—the TRUTH OR DARE parties we hosted, VIP guests at ROCK CONCERTS and BABYSITTING for GRANDKIDS.

1208. I love that New Year is the only holiday that celebrates Time—it's the Planet's Birthday.

1209. I love to gather with friends on New Year's Eve and play NEW YEAR'S QUEST.•

1210. Even though it's winter, I love collecting beautiful loves on the shore of my life.

1211. I love that to become the PEARL, I have to embrace the SAND.

1212. I love the upwelling of gratitude I feel when I count my blessings.

1213. I love that by keeping last year's crazy New Year's resolution to "beat the drum for love" I discovered a secret to happiness.

• Joy created *New Year's Quest* to harness the energies of "new beginnings" everyone feels around New Years. Since the questions we ask determine the quest we take, the nearly 50 questions are designed to help people take stock of the year that's passed and visualize the year to come so they create their best year yet.

The moment you have in your heart this extraordinary thing called love and feel the depth, the delight, the ecstasy of it, you will discover that for you the world is transformed.

— Krishnamurti

Creating Heaven on Earth

Religions proclaim a Heaven or Paradise that exists somewhere else, and claim to have the only map to get there.

A simpler truth may be that we create our own heaven but on earth. Love by love....

Love by Love we lay the foundation....

Love by love we build the bridge....

When we love everything that happens in our life, perhaps we'll enter what's been called the Kingdom of Heaven.

And a child will lead them...

Perhaps a child's game is the secret....

The more of our life we can love, the more we'll be living in the Kingdom of Heaven.

The more of our life we love, the more everything will reveal itself as a miracle.

And the more we can love, the more we will attract even more things to love.

And in the end the love you take

is equal to the love you make

— the Beatles

Part 3

Epilogue

January - April 2013

I'm including some of my *LoveSpells* for the first few months of 2013 because it was during this period that I finally moved from LA to LI.

The Dreaded Move

In early January I returned to LA to pack for the move across the country before escrow closed the first week of February. For a few nights before I left Long Island, I lay awake dreading my return to LA and what lay ahead.

Besides the emotional ordeal, there were the logistics of packing—choosing what to take and what to leave and what to give away, orchestrating family members coming by to choose things they wanted to keep. What would I do with the rest? Donate? Estate sale? Sell my car? Let's not forget hiring a reputable moving company. And I had only thirty days to deal with the 1001 details. How would I get it all done in time?

Lilly planned on joining me in a few weeks, but the major portion of sorting through everything, organizing and packing had to be done alone.

From the moment I landed in LA, I put one foot in front of the other, added to and checked off my To Do list. Once again I discovered that contemplating the unknown is more stressful than simply dealing with what has to be done. Though the task seemed impossible, day after day I made slow but steady progress.

During the day I was too busy to worry, and at night I was too tired to stress. I did what I could every day, working until late into the evening. Yet, as had become my habit, I found a few minutes to cast a *LoveSpell*.

1214. I love an 80-degree day today in January—makes leaving LA so much harder.

1215. As I prepare to move from LA to LI, I love being willing to "let go" of my stuff.

1216. I love giving away things rather than throwing them out so they'll be used and appreciated by others.

1217. I love scissors—an ingenious technology—especially when I'm packing to move.

1218. I love having the courage to let go of an old life—friends, community (it's not easy!)—so I can embrace a new one.

1219. I love re-reading the loving inscriptions in the books I've received as gifts over the years before giving them away.

1220. I love knowing I'm not my stuff—otherwise this move would feel like an amputation.

1221. On my birthday I love the life I've lived, I'm living, and the life I have yet to live!

Our LoveSpell

Alone on my birthday, rooting around in storage, sorting through the debris of the life I'd lived with Joy. I could have easily sunk into a pity party.

So you can imagine how good it felt to return from storage and find a FedEx package on my doorstep. To my surprise, it was a birthday gift from Lilly—she'd sent me *Our LoveSpell: 10 Things I Love About Loving You.*

I'd just published it as a way to focus the insight of the *LoveSpell Secret* on one's relationships. It's a perfect present for birthdays or Valentine's Day. After all, what greater gift can you give the people in your life than to tell them what you love about them?!

Reading all the things Lilly loved about me lifted my spirits! Not only as the recipient but also as the author! I felt firsthand how wonderful it was to receive such a gift!

On January 22nd Lilly flew to LA to help me finish packing. Since we'd been apart on my birthday, we planned a belated celebration. The very next day we drove two hours to our favorite spa, Two Bunch Palms, in Desert Hot Springs for some sorely needed R&R. Besides the emotional drain, packing had also been a physical strain. In the past we'd stayed a week, but this time we could only stay for two nights.

1222. I love how my TweetHeart has flown to LA to help me.

1223. I love being felt by my Tweetheart's sculptor's hands.

1224. I love floating in water especially in the hot springs of Two Bunch Palms.

1225. I love watching a waterfall and hearing its soothing symphony of rushing water.

1226. I love slowing down so much I can see the clouds forming & reforming in the sky.

1227. I love receiving a massage—especially after straining my back lifting boxes in preparation for my move.

1228. I love the sensation of lying naked in a hot spring pool catching raindrops in my mouth.

1229. I love how my TweetHeart "goes savage" on me when we make love.

1230. I love those rare moments of abandon when I forget who I am, even that I'm human.

An Oasis in the Chaos A Haven in the Storm

Those weeks in January packing up my life in LA were some of the most stressful and exhausting I can recall. And yet, casting *LoveSpells* was like a refuge, my "sacred pause," an oasis in the chaos, a haven in the storm.

In the midst of comparing moving company bids, interviewing Estate Sales professionals, scheduling various required inspections, negotiating with the prospective buyer, shredding documents, contacting power, water and cable utilities to cancel my account, and attending to the myriad details my move required, I cast *LoveSpells*.

Had this move occurred the previous January, when I'd just begun casting *LoveSpells,* I doubt I would have been able to keep it up. But more than a year along—my *LoveHabit* ingrained, my *LoveMuscle* strong—casting *LoveSpells* was the familiar ground I retreated to as I found myself increasingly uprooted and disoriented, a stranger in what had once been my home.

Surrounded by cardboard boxes, packing tape, bubble wrap and the increasing chaos that resulted from packing, I continued to find things to love.

1231. I love watching the skills master movers & estate sale-ers apply to their work.

1232. I love bubble wrap & banker boxes & packing tape.

1233. I love that I can laugh now at a lot of things that used to make me cry.

1234. I love looking ahead with what I'll call "curiosity" instead of "anxiety."

1235. I love twisties and rubber bands to tie up the electrical cords from all my computers.

1236. I love taking a break from packing with a cafe au lait basking in the afternoon sun.

1237. I love saying goodbye to my things knowing how much lighter I'm going to feel. Enlightened?

1238. I love the awareness that Time is both an enemy & a friend, and being able to discriminate between the two.

1239. I love falling into bed after a long exhausting day of packing.

Letting Go

Part of the frenzy of the packing-move was squeezing in the time to say goodbye to dear friends. Every encounter was filled with emotion—deep exchanges of gratitude. I gave thanks and received thanks, the kind often reserved for one's memorial. It was a death of sorts—my life in LA was over.

So amidst the packing, taping and bubble-wrapping, I was engaged in a long, emotional goodbye with the people and city I loved. My eyes continually watered with tears at the slightest provocation. Perhaps because I was filled with both gratitude and grief

At the last minute, the sale of my home fell through. I was too busy packing to spend much time worrying about it. Within 24 hours my realtor had backup offers.

1240. I love getting the chance to thank someone who's made a difference in my life.

1241. I love having lived somewhere long enough so I have many people to say hello to on my daily rounds.

1242. I love when a friend thanks me for saving them from "drowning" during a stormy period of their life.

1243. I love having lived near a lake for the past dozen years—what a blessing!

1244. I love being able to tear up in empathy when an old friend shares the intimate wound of profound loss.

1245. To my surprise I love visiting old haunts in LA one last time to say goodbye.

1246. I love telling someone how important and helpful they were to me during a dark passage in my life.

The Last Goodbye

Showering on the morning of the move, I noticed something on the bottom of the tub. When I picked it up to see what it was, I gasped.

Years earlier, for our first Valentine's Day together. I had given Joy a gold anklet inscribed with our names. She had never taken it off.

After Joy breathed her last, I took the delicate chain from her ankle and wrapped it around my left wrist. I wore it ever since, So on the morning of my move from our home—standing in the shower, holding the broken anklet—I was stunned.

It wasn't only that this precious keepsake had broken, it was also the incredible synchronicity—as if Joy knew that our home was no more and was releasing me so I could move on and fully embrace my new life.

A chill ran through me and tears spilled from my eyes as I absorbed the significance of what had happened. I had no idea there would be another even more astonishing sign from Joy yet to come.

1247. I love how after the movers left, as I sat on the floor of our completely empty home, memories of my life with Joy came flooding back.

1248. I love being able to LET GO OF MY OLD LIFE so I can EMBRACE THE NEW LIFE that awaits me.

1249. I love that my move is finally over—I deserve a vacation!

1250. I love having nothing to do after weeks of packing & moving—Ahh!

1251. I love being able to travel from balmy weather & swaying palm trees to frigid snowdrifts in just a few hours.

1252. I love how the "Easy" button I packed kept repeating THAT WAS EASY! with every bump of the road all the way home from the airport.

1253. I love Oliver Wendell Holmes' quote—"Where we love is home, home that our feet may leave, but not our hearts."

That Was Easy!

Lilly and I left a balmy LA, with temperatures in the 70's, and arrived in freezing New York around midnight where we had to contend with two feet of snow.

To our surprise, during the forty-minute cab ride from the airport, we were serenaded by the Easy Button.

Throughout the packing ordeal, I'd used the Easy Button—which, when pressed, utters a congratulatory "That was easy!"—for humor and encouragement. It had been one of the last things I threw in the suitcase and was lying on the bottom of one of the bags in the back of the cab. Every bump in the road triggered a "That was easy!" as if the universe was acknowledging how hard the move had been and how well we'd done.

When we arrived at Lilly's home in the middle of the night, we faced one final hurdle: Lilly's driveway hadn't been ploughed and 3-foot snowdrifts blocked the front door. After dragging four heavy suitcases through hip-high drifts and then digging our way into the house, we collapsed in hysterical laughter amidst piles of melting snow. Though exhausted and wet, I was elated—my move was over and I was home.

1254. I love the resilience of my body that can heal after the wear & tear & strain of packing & moving cross-country.

1255. I love throwing snowballs to my dog—a rare delight for someone who's lived in LA.

1256. I love giving Lilly "Our LoveSpell" for Valentine's Day and telling her 10 things (more like a 100) I love about her.

1257. I love how well I'm adjusting to this Change of Address—I wonder if casting LoveSpells is part of the reason?

1258. I love the countdown to Spring in a way I never felt in LA—23 days to go!

1259. I love anticipating the new perspectives a different climate & environment will give me.

1260. I love Henry Miller's line—One's destination is never a place but a new way of seeing things.

The Final Sign

Adjusting to a bitterly cold New York winter was only one of many challenges I faced after my move from LA to LI. Another had to do with the sale of my home.

Since the backup buyer also dropped out, my realtor informed me that without furniture, my home wouldn't show as well as it had when it was filled with our tasteful décor. Empty, it clearly needed new paint, carpeting, even lighting that would cost thousands of dollars. Once the renovation was complete, the place had to be staged—temporarily furnished and decorated to give potential buyers a vision of what it could be. Another significant expense.

Ultimately, the effort and expense paid off. The home Joy and I had lived in finally sold on Friday, April 5th the last business day before the 6-year anniversary of Joy's passing on April 6th. Of all the days in the year! What an incredible synchronicity! What a sign!

Fifteen months earlier on that fateful New Year's Eve, Joy asked me *What do you love?* Her question propelled me on a quest that taught me the *LoveSpell Secret*. By inspiring this *LoveSpell Experiment*, was Joy preparing me for the uprooting and upheaval I'd have to endure if I was to going create a new life with Lilly?

1261. I love waking up to a chorus of birdsong—especially after a long, cold & quiet winter.

1262. I love the idea of having a "bubble wrap party" when my stuff arrives from LA.

1263. I love sitting in the sun—soaking up the Vitamin D—after a long, dark winter.

1264. I love decorating my new home in LI with cherished momentos from LA.

1265. I love today—the sun is out and it's the 1st Day of Spring!

1266. I love that, though it's snowing on the 2nd day of Spring, I'm not depressed—just wondering when Nature will get its act together?

1267. I love that the best things in life are unseen—maybe that's why we close our eyes when we kiss, dream and pray.

1268. I love this "gift" of uprooting & moving — discovering that I'm "home" wherever I am.

Some day, after we have mastered the winds,
the waves, the tides and gravity,
we shall harness the energies of love.
Then, for the second time in the history of the world,
mankind will have discovered fire.

— Teilhard de Chardin

Part 4

The Results

The Experiment's Results

As it turned out, 2012 was a relatively "good" year: a mix of highs and lows that included deteriorating vision due to retinal problems and the major upheaval of my move from LA to LI. I'm grateful that I faced nothing as traumatic as a major illness or a death. I know what those kinds of years are like.

I have no doubt that casting a *LoveSpell* every day kept my spirits up despite the stress of bi-coastal living out of a suitcase for a good part of the year. My habit of focusing on what I love stood me in good stead when I suffered the after-effects of Hurricane Sandy. Even during the stressful ordeal of moving, I found things to love.

The results of my *LoveSpell Experiment* may not have been dramatic, but they were profound, My life has changed. Or rather, my view of my life has changed, and that makes all the difference.

I continue *to beat the drum for love* and cast a *LoveSpell* every day, and don't see myself stopping any time soon. Why would I stop when it feels so good and I receive so many benefits from my daily dose of Vitamin L?

What did I learn from my LoveSpell Experiment?

Besides mining my life for the gold of the things I love, and depositing more than 1001 loves in my *LoveBank*, I got to know myself in new ways.

Beyond deriving the quantum benefits that come from focusing on what I love, I developed the habit of looking at my life through "love-colored glasses" and the view has been amazing!

During *My Year of Casting 1001 LoveSpells*, I've learned what it means to *Occupy My Heart* and discovered these three fundamental truths:

1. *The great challenge of life is to love as much as you can, to* Love Everything!
2. *The great remedy/medicine/Rx for what ails you—for what's wrong with your life—is to* Love Everything*!*
3. *The great secret of life, indeed the secret to happiness, is to* Love Everything*!*

"What do you love?"

is a four-word question that could change the world.

Blessed are those who Occupy Their Heart

and engage the world in a Love-o-lution.

— I. J. Weinstock

It's Your Turn

I've shared my *LoveSpell Experiment* because it's been such a positive and transformative experience for me. I hope it will inspire you to conduct your own *LoveSpell Experiment* so you can create more love in your life, reap the amazing quantum benefits, and discover yourself in new and wonderful ways.

If you are inspired, my workbook—The LoveSpell Secret: *A 30-Day Heaven-Sent Program to Create More Love in Your Life* —is the place to begin.

May your life be filled with love

And may you fill the world with that love!

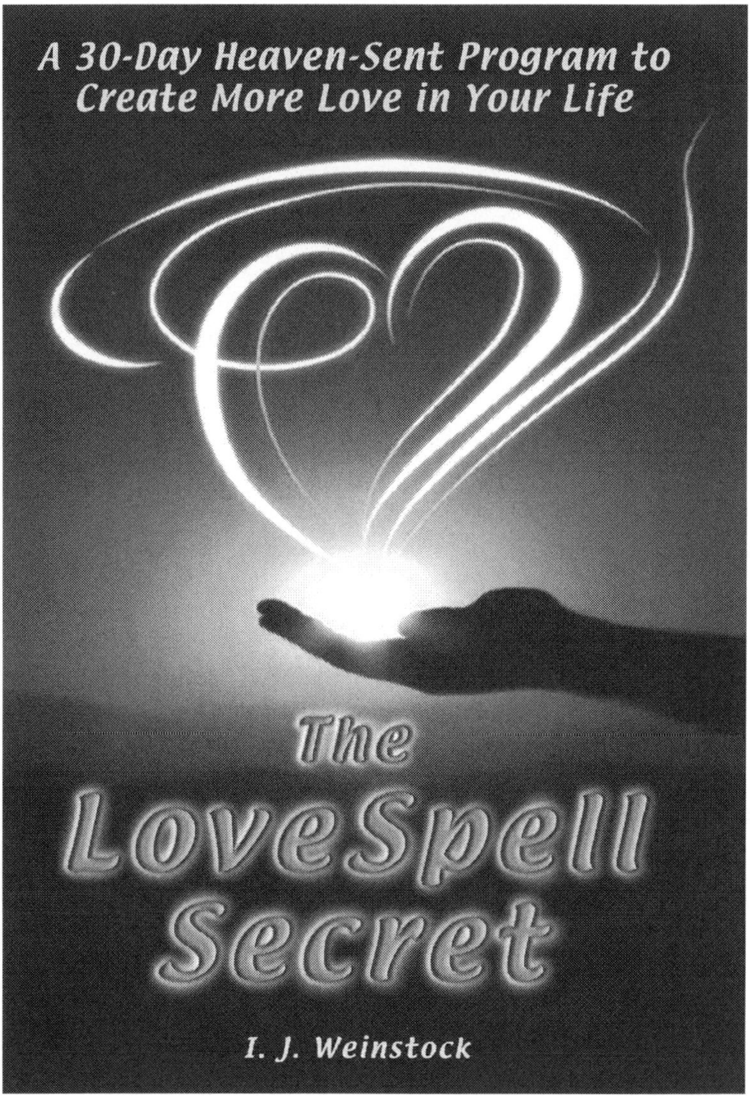
A 30-Day Heaven-Sent Program to Create More Love in Your Life
The LoveSpell Secret
I. J. Weinstock

The LoveSpell Secret

A 30-Day Heaven-Sent Program to Create More Love in Your Life

Inspired by my ***LoveSpell Experiment,*** I've created a workbook, **The LoveSpell Secret: *A 30-Day Heaven-Sent Program to Create More Love in Your Life,*** to help you develop the habit of asking and answering one of life's most important questions—*What do you love?*

To actually grow the love in your life, you can't just read about it, you have to do it. If you do it for the next 30 days—*Acknowledge*, *Appreciate* and pay *Attention* to the love in your life—you'll develop the habit of looking at your life through love-colored glasses, receive the amazing benefits of your increased dose of *Vitamin L*, and discover that the power to grow the love in your life is in your heart and in your hands.

> *"What do you love?"* What a profound and necessary question. Thanks for reminding us to ask the question on a regular basis. To paraphrase the wisdom in this handbook, I think we'd all do well to acknowledge, appreciate and pay attention to this guide!
>
> *— Dr. Seth Kadish*
>
> *"Pop Your Patterns: The No-Nonsense Way to Change Your Life"*

On Valentine's Day

Give Someone You Love the Gift of

Our LoveSpell

During my **LoveSpell Experiment,** I discovered the magic of asking one of life's most important questions—*What do you love?* Whenever you answer that question, you benefit from the proven quantum effect that expands whatever you focus on, literally growing the love in your life.

Our **LoveSpell:** ***10 Things I Love About Loving You*** is the perfect Valentine's Day gift that you and your loved one will treasure forever because the greatest gift you can give someone is to tell them what you love about them.

Our LoveSpell will help you do just that. Complete the 10 questions about what you love about that special person in your life. Your answers will "amplify and magnify" your love. And the person with whom you share **Our LoveSpell** will receive a precious & priceless gift.

Coming Soon for **CHILDREN...**

A new children's game brings real magic
into children's lives.

How do you play the **LoveSpell Game**?

Simply answer the question *What do you love?*

When you think of something you love you feel good.

So the more you love, the better you feel
and the more you win!

The LoveSpell Game

The More You Love, The More You Win!

The *LoveSpell Game* is so simple even a child can do it. In fact, children should do it—it's as important for them as learning to brush their teeth. Parents who play the *LoveSpell Game* with their children at the kitchen table, in the car, or while putting them to bed, are teaching their children the habit of focusing on what they love and giving them an invaluable life-skill.

The *LoveSpell Game* is not only fun, it's good for you! When children play the *LoveSpell Game*, they receive the scientifically-proven benefits of *Vitamin L.* Children who develop the habit of playing the *LoveSpell Game* will reap the amazing benefits for the rest of their lives.

The *LoveSpell Game* will be introduced in three soon-to-be-published children's book series:

The Secret of the LoveSpell Fairies

The Magic Glasses

The LoveSpell Game

JOYride

How My Late Wife Loved Me Back To Life

Joy and Jerry were soulmates, in fact, they were literally a "match-made-in heaven" according to Joy's channeled memoir, **Love Ever After**.

When Jerry lost Joy to breast cancer, he was devastated. Then a remarkable thing happened—Joy began communicating with him from the Afterlife and led him on an incredible journey to heal his grief. Ultimately, like the final scene in the movie, *Ghost,* Joy found someone, a willing medium, through whom she literally loved him back to life.

"Most people will be shocked by our story. I can't blame them. I'd heard of life-after-death, but sex-after-death? If I hadn't experienced it myself, I wouldn't have believed it either. But this is a true story. It happened to me." ~ **I. J. Weinstock**, from the Introduction

JOYride is as fantastic a love story as the hit movie, *Ghost*, except it's REAL! This book will change the way you view life, death, love and what is possible.

Love Ever After

How My Husband Became My Spirit Guide
by Joy Mitchell Lisker (I. J. Weinstock's late wife)

It all began with a murder!...

In 1983 Bob Lisker suffered a tragedy of biblical proportions. His wife, Dorka, had been brutally murdered in their Los Angeles home and his teenage son, Bruce, despite pleas of innocence, was convicted of the crime and sentenced to life in prison.

Tormented by the loss of his wife and his only son, this conservative attorney, former Marine and pillar of the community attempted to contact the spirit of his dead wife to find out who killed her. This set the stage for the extraordinary Afterlife communications his 2nd wife, Joy Mitchell Lisker, received after he died.

According to Joy, Bob Lisker was the least likely candidate to be a spirit guide. Yet from the moment he left his body, he gave her a guided tour of the Afterlife that included:

- What happens when we die
- How spirits live and learn on the Other Side
- Reincarnation and the illusion of time
- How the soul chooses its lessons
- How to contact your loved ones on the Other Side
- How to recognize your life path
- How to attract money
- Bob's 12-step program to realize your dreams

This 10th anniversary edition includes an Afterword by Joy's surviving husband, I. J. Weinstock, entitled "The Joyful Redemption" that describes Bruce Lisker's 2009 exoneration and release from prison as seen on the TV show 48 Hours.

JOYride: *How My Late Wife Loved Me Back to Life*, I. J. Weinstock's award-winning grief memoir, is the companion sequel to **Love Ever After**.

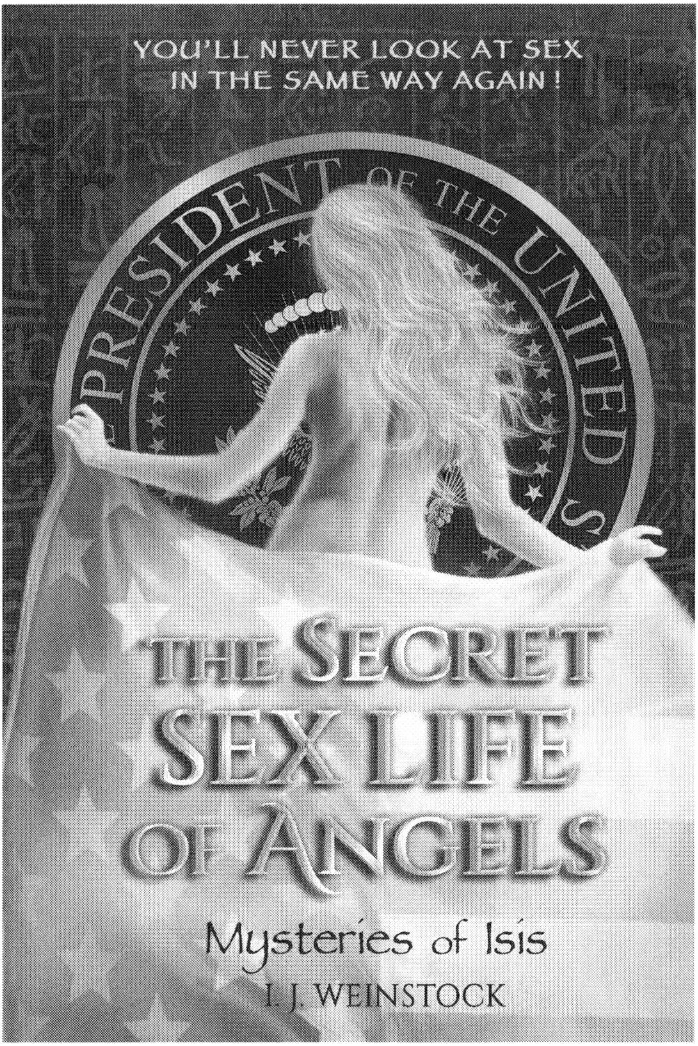
YOU'LL NEVER LOOK AT SEX IN THE SAME WAY AGAIN !
PRESIDENT OF THE UNITED S
THE SECRET SEX LIFE OF ANGELS
Mysteries of Isis
I. J. WEINSTOCK

The Secret Sex Life of Angels

by I. J Weinstock

In a world with no future, one man is offered a secret key from the past to unlock the greatest mystery of all.

On the 100th day of his presidency, Adam Hart discovers that to fulfill his oath of office he must embark on a sexual odyssey that could determine the fate of the world.

The Secret Sex Life of Angels combines the intrigue and controversy of *The Da Vinci Code* with the spirituality and eroticism of the *Kama Sutra* in a fantastic saga about the sacred nature of sex.

"Every man needs to read *The Secret Sex Life of Angels.* Every woman needs to have her man read this book."

"You'll never think about sex in the same way again!"

"This is the book everyone will be talking about."

Acknowledgements

Every labor of love has many hands and hearts.

I want to thank April Hope Owen for hosting the New Year's Eve drum circle where I heard Joy's question—*What do you love?*

I am deeply indebted to Dana Julien for throwing me into the Twitter pool, confident that I'dlearn to swim-tweet, which gave me a perfect medium for *beating the drum for love.*

I can't sing Dehanna Bailee's praises enough—she's every author's dream "book shepherd."

I learned to love from my family and friends to whom I am deeply indebted. And I'm especially grateful to my brother Steven Weinstock—the most generous man I know—who always has my back so I can devote more of myself to exploring love.

And finally, my profoundest gratitude goes to my TweetHeart, Lilly Julien, for holding my hand and heart, for her support and inspiration, and for the 1001 new things she's taught me about love.

About the Author

I. J. "Jerry" Weinstock is the son of Holocaust survivors. During his varied career, he's been an actor, artist, producer and author. In the 80's, his groundbreaking book about women was featured on the *Donahue Show* (the Oprah of its time). In the 90's, his cable network, The Game Channel, was the precursor to GSN (The Game Show Network).

When Jerry lost his wife, Joy, to breast cancer, he was devastated. But a remarkable thing happened—Joy began communicating with him from the Afterlife. Over the course of a year, she led him on an incredible journey to heal his grief. Inspired by his experience, he wrote, *JOYride: How My Late Wife Loved Me Back To Life.*

On New Year's Eve 2011, while participating in a drum circle, Joy once again communicated with him. She asked him a simple yet profound question—*What do you love?*—which became the inspiration for *The LoveSpell Experiment: My Year Exploring Love & Discovering A Secret To Happiness.* He is also the author of *The LoveSpell Secret: A 30-Day Heaven-Sent Program to Create More Love in Your Life.*

When not leading workshops at bereavement conferences about healing from grief, or giving talks about the *LoveSpell Secret* and how to create more love in your life, I. J. Weinstock writes speculative fiction.

In **ULTRA BOWL**—a sci-fi adventure fable about football, robots and time-travel—he explores the dangers of our Digital Age and the dystopian future toward which we may be heading.

In ***The Secret Sex Life of Angels,*** he writes about the magic and mystery of sacred sexuality.

I. J. Weinstock lives on Long Island, New York, with his TweetHeart Lilly, where he spends his time loving more and more of his life and inspiring others to join the *Love-O-lution*. He can be reached at DreaMasterBooks@gmail.com or on Twitter @SoulmateGuider. For more information, visit his website www.IJWeinstock.com.

27079468R00157

Printed in Poland
by Amazon Fulfillment
Poland Sp. z o.o., Wrocław